DEREK MAHON

DEREK MAHON

A Study of His Poetry

CHRISTOPHER STEARE

Greenwich Exchange
London

Greenwich Exchange, London

First published in Great Britain in 2017
All rights reserved

Derek Mahon: A Study of His Poetry
© Christopher Steare, 2017

Printed and bound by imprintdigital.com
Cover design by December Publications
Tel: 07951511275

Greenwich Exchange Website: www.greenex.co.uk

Cataloguing in Publication Data is available
from the British Library

ISBN: 978-1-910996-08-9

for Michèle and Hannah

CONTENTS

Preface

READERS COMING TO DEREK MAHON FOR the first time face a number of difficulties. For a start the sheer range of allusions in his poetry – to other poems and poets, artists, places, cultures, historical events – makes any poem 'a forest of intertextuality', to borrow Mahon's own phrase (itself an allusion to Baudelaire's 'forest of symbols'). Not since Eliot has a poet so honeycombed his work with borrowings, thefts, direct or indirect quotations, other languages, multiple voices. The effect is sometimes that of collage, bric-a-brac, a cut-and-paste poetics that runs the risk of fragmentation. That Mahon's poetry generally avoids such a fate is a sign of the guiding intelligence behind it, and readers soon begin to see that Mahon's poetry, for all its fissiparous energies, returns again and again to a few insistent and persistent themes: the experience of exile, art as resistance to modernity, the aesthetics of waste.

The other potential cause of confusion is a textual one. The publishing history of Mahon's poetry is complicated by a bewildering indeterminacy. Many poems have, over the past forty years, been subject to some fairly radical changes. Poems have been retitled, expanded, cut or dropped altogether from later collected editions, a revisionist poetics that calls into question the whole concept of canonicity. (For this reason I have chosen to base this study on the 2011 *New Collected Poems* as representing the most recent form in which Mahon wishes his poems to be published). Yet what looks like a somewhat cavalier approach to his own *oeuvre* is, as we shall see, a resistance to anything set too firmly in stone, a way of destabilising the poem and our response to it in order to be true to the shifting, contingent nature of life itself. As Mahon himself says, adopting the voice of Heraclitus, philosopher of flux:

> You will tell me that you have executed
> A monument more lasting than bronze;
> But even bronze is perishable.
> Your best poem, you know the one I mean,
> The very language in which the poem
> Was written, and the idea of language,
> All these things will pass away in time.
> – *from* 'Heraclitus on Rivers'

Or to put it another way: you never step into the same poem twice.

1

Night-Crossing (1968)

THE SPRING OF 1966 SAW THE publication of Seamus Heaney's first collection of poems, *Death of a Naturalist*. In 1968 Derek Mahon's first volume, *Night-Crossing*, was published, following the poet's return to Ireland after two years in Canada and the USA. In 1969 Michael Longley – Mahon's closest friend at that time – brought out his own first collection, *No Continuing City*. The convergence of these three Ulster poets at a critical period in Northern Ireland's history inevitably tempted commentators to refer to a Northern Irish Renaissance, a cross-fertilising of gifts that had not been seen since the Irish Literary Revival of the late 19th and early 20th centuries. As with that earlier movement, the forging of a new Irish poetic identity in the 1960s took place against a background of increased political tension. *Night-Crossing* came out in the same year as the Troubles began, and the sudden outbreak of sectarian violence coincided with Mahon's return to what he describes in his opening poem 'Spring in Belfast' as 'this desperate city'. Nearly all of the poems in *Night-Crossing* were written before the Troubles broke, yet a sense of unease pervades the volume, as if at any minute the political weather might turn.

If the shadow of violence falls over all of these three first collections, the spirit of friendship and poetic rivalry sustains them. Derek Mahon and Michael Longley were contemporaries at Trinity College Dublin, living in typical student squalor and trading apprentice poems over pints. Some of Mahon's earliest poems were published in undergraduate magazines and it was at Trinity that he began to cultivate the image of the bohemian poet, 'a surly *étranger* in a donkey jacket, with literary pretensions' as he later portrayed himself. Yet it was their common background in Belfast that did more than anything to bring Mahon and Longley together. In his poem 'Letter to Derek Mahon', Longley pays affectionate tribute to his fellow Belfast poet, describing the pair of them as 'two poetic conservatives/In the city of guns and long knives'. It was also in Belfast, under the aegis of Philip Hobsbaum at Queen's University, that Mahon and Longley established a lasting friendship with Seamus Heaney.

The closeness between the three young poets is caught in a group photograph of the time: Longley and Mahon stand side by side, with Heaney a little apart on the right. The photograph is instructive, however, because of the presence behind them of another, older Northern Irish poet, John Hewitt. Hewitt is important to an understanding of Derek Mahon's poetry, if only for negative reasons. Hewitt had consistently argued that the Ulster poet must define himself by his Ulster inheritance. 'The Ulster writer must be a rooted man,' he wrote. 'He must carry the native tang of his idiom like the native dust on his sleeve; otherwise he is an airy internationalist, thistledown, a twig in the stream'. In a review in the *Irish Times* of Hewitt's selected prose (a volume called, significantly, *Ancestral Voices*) Mahon's response to this prescriptive view of Ulster poetry was good-humoured but robust:

> This is a bit tough on thistledown; and speaking as a twig in a stream, I feel there's a certain harshness, a dogmatism at work there.

Mahon might also have accepted the label of 'airy internationalist', given the global reach of much of his poetry. Interestingly, in the same group photograph, it is Hewitt who is holding the traditional pipe while Mahon seems to be clutching a sheaf of newspapers. Already at this stage in his career Mahon is looking impatiently out at the world, hungry for news beyond his native Belfast. In fact, Hewitt's insistence that a poet should 'have *ancestors*' resonates more in the context of Heaney's poetry than Mahon's. Heaney's background as a Catholic from County Derry, his sense of belonging to a beleaguered nationalist minority, his understanding of the oppressive weight of Irish history, and 'the exact/and tribal intimate revenge' of sectarianism, all contrast with Mahon's reluctance to define himself as anything other than – as he would later put it – 'A recovering Ulster Protestant from County Down'. Edna Longley, Michael Longley's wife and a fellow student with Mahon in Dublin, encapsulated Mahon's position in a satirical clerihew, published in *The Honest Ulsterman* in 1975:

> DEREK MAHON
> Is doing all he can
> To rid his imagination
> Of the Northern Irish situation.

If Heaney's poetry is inherently *centripetal*, a quest for origins, an attempt – as he puts it in 'Personal Helicon' – to 'pry into roots, to finger slime,/To stare, big-eyed Narcissus, into some spring', then Mahon's poetry is *centrifugal*, taking him away from the centre to the circumference in a continual journeying out into various states of exile. This sense of displacement from the centre – wherever that may be – is very powerful in Mahon's work. For example, in 'Bird Sanctuary', the speaker occupies a liminal position at the shoreline of consciousness, on the edge of a waking dream. Only here can the poet build the imagined bird sanctuary that will 'hold/The loaded world in check', the word 'loaded' being itself loaded, triggering images of guns and ammunition. The contrast between the ecstatic world of the birds and his own life 'elsewhere' is made painfully acute in the third stanza where the 'city down the coast' is described as 'composed of earth and fire'. This oblique reference to Belfast underlines the poet's need to escape into the sanctuary of song, an impulse towards aestheticism that will come to dominate Mahon's restless, fugitive art.

Other poems in *Night-Crossing* that enact a journey out include 'Day Trip to Donegal' – where postcard memories of a visit to the West Coast blend into a dream narrative that situates the speaker 'at dawn ... alone far out at sea' – and 'An Unborn Child', where the experience of exile is dramatised in the context of the child's expulsion from the womb. Adopting the voice of an embryonic consciousness, the speaker displays a vivid awareness both of itself – 'I am completely egocentric' – and the 'familiar room' it is about to 'vacate'. The sense of security felt by the foetus is threatened by a proleptic intuition of 'the splitting light above/My head' and that, even as it cries out for life, its days are already 'numbered'. The word 'numbered' not only carries in its Biblical echoes a projected sense of end-time but also plays on notions of numbness, of a loss of feeling and an estrangement – a 'splitting' – from the natural environment of the mother's eco-system.

This separation from nature as the child learns to adapt to the world is a cause of intense anxiety in many of the poems in *Night-Crossing* and will become a dominant trope in Mahon's work as a whole. In 'Breton Walks', for example, after an imaginative recreation of creation itself – 'a cold day breaking on silent stones' – the cosmic setting

of the first section, 'Morning', is disrupted by the
appearance first of an old woman – more archetype than
real – and then, in the second section, 'Man and Bird', by
the figure of the speaker himself. His attempt to summon
the birds with 'whistle-talk' fails every time, leaving him
painfully conscious of 'the gap/From their world to the
world of men'. The poem darkens as it moves through the
day and into night. The speaker's voice in the third section
'After Midnight' now becomes suspicious, almost paranoid,
as he imagines the 'beasts of the field, birds of the air,/
Their slit-eyes glittering everywhere' and concludes:

> I am man self-made, self-made man,
> No small-talk now for those who ran
>
> In and out of my grubby childhood.
> We have grown up as best we could.

   A note of preening self-sufficiency is caught in the phrase
'man self-made, self-made man' where the chiasmus
performs the dialectic of self-creation it describes. The
hubris, however, is tempered by melancholy as the poet
recognises that the 'small-talk' which in childhood had
connected him to the animals has been silenced as 'shades
of the prison house' – to borrow a familiar image from
Wordsworth – begin to close upon him. The poem's fourth
and final section, 'Exit Molloy', continues the allegory of
isolation into the grave itself as the poet, in the persona of
Beckett's eponymous anti-hero, lies wintering in 'a dark

ditch', exiled from 'the little town only a mile away'. The cycle of alienation is complete as a bell tolls and a disembodied voice utters its final consolatory couplet:

> Strictly speaking I am already dead
> But still I can hear the birds sing on over my head.

The extended last line has the effect of a temporary release from the *rigor mortis* of pentameter rhythm as the egocentric 'I' of the poem (there are ten uses of the first person in the space of nine lines) dissolves in an epiphany of bird song.

Beckett's work was an important influence on Mahon's poetry ever since he took a year out from Trinity College to study at the Sorbonne in Paris. It was here that he continued to project himself as a belated *poète maudit*, smoking Gauloises and reading Camus and Sartre – as well as the French Symbolists – in the cafés of the Latin Quarter. Such studies, however, form only a part of a hinterland of influences that has shaped Mahon's work and the range of allusions to other writers and artists in his poetry has been extensive. One reason why Mahon's poetry has not, perhaps, penetrated the public imagination – in the way that Heaney's poetry has – could be the dense intertextuality of the poems. Yet the references are always for the sake of a deeper understanding of his poetic vocation, a way of measuring himself against those whose status as outsiders, as intellectual vagrants of one kind or another, speaks to his own self-alienation.

In *Night-Crossing* two such figures are Thomas De Quincey and Vincent van Gogh. In 'De Quincey at Grasmere' Mahon provides a portrait of the Romantic essayist, autobiographer and self-proclaimed addict, whose pursuit of the 'seventh heaven' induced by laudanum, together with his restless wanderings in London, provide a 19th-century equivalent to the peregrinating sensibility that Mahon himself was beginning to develop. De Quincey's quest for a 'panacea' for the anguish induced by mental and geographical displacement is also one of the earliest analogues in Mahon's poetry for the search for an 'artificial paradise' that might compensate for the lack of an 'authentic' life. As Stephen Enniss demonstrates in his recent biography of Mahon, that search would have far-reaching personal consequences, including the break-up of his marriage, psychiatric hospitalisation and an increasingly destructive dependence on alcohol.

In 'A Portrait of the Artist' a similar displacement is explored in an imagined letter from Vincent van Gogh to his brother Theo. The artist has not yet become the painter of cornfields and starry nights, but is still 'shivering in the darkness/Of pits, slag-heaps, turnip fields'. It is tempting to see van Gogh's subterranean life as an equivalent to the buried life in Belfast that some of Mahon's early poems describe and stubbornly resist. The artist/poet is compared to 'a caged bird in springtime/Banging the bright bars' or 'a glow-worm ... among/The caged Belgian miners'. The image of van Gogh's Davy lamp as 'the dying light of faith' invites a reading that might link the collapsing of religious belief into aesthetics – 'God gutters down to metaphor'– with the poet's own reconfiguring of his Ulster Protestant past into poetry. Artist and poet become, by necessity, exiles both from traditional forms of faith and also from that physical and metaphysical 'North' where such forms are most rigidly entrenched. 'In time,' the speaker says, 'I shall go south/And paint what I have seen'. The poem ends in a secular transfiguration as the objects of the painter's vision – 'chairs, faces and old boots' – are invested with a numinous light until the caged miners themselves return in the form of sunflowers and fishing boats.

'A Portrait of the Artist' may be read as an early indicator of Mahon's search for an exit strategy that will release him from 'the Northern Irish situation' into something like Keats's Mediterranean pastoral in 'Ode to a Nightingale', a place where he might drink from 'a beaker full of the warm south'. However, there are other poems in *Night-Crossing* which acknowledge, albeit reluctantly, a gravitational pull back into the city of his birth, to that matrix where, as he wryly and ambiguously notes in 'Spring in Belfast', 'one part of my mind must learn to know its place.'

In 'Glengormley', for example, (originally published as 'Suburban Walk') Mahon offers a severely diminished view of his native city. The poem conveys a strong sense of historical and cultural shrinkage as the opening quotation from Sophocles's *Antigone* – 'Wonders are many and none is more wonderful than man' – sets up large-scale, mythic expectations that are immediately cut down to size by the bathos of the lines that follow: 'Who has tamed the terrier, trimmed the hedge/And grasped the principle of the watering can'. To be born into suburbia is – the poem implies – to occupy a world trimmed of heroic grandeur or tragic significance. Taming the *terrier* becomes a synecdoche for modern Ireland's efforts to insulate itself from ancient *terrors*, to keep itself 'safe from monsters, and the giants/Who tore up sods twelve miles by six/And hurled them out to sea to become islands'. Such founding myths, we are told, 'Can worry us no more'. The neutral, detached register of the poem reflects the blandness of the world it surveys, a world where 'No saint or hero,/Landing at night from the conspiring seas,/Brings dangerous tokens to the new era'. Yet although the poet colludes, ironically, in the banishment of saints and heroes from contemporary Ireland, the violence encoded in Ulster legends resurfaces in diluted form in the bitter language of political discourse: 'Only words hurt us now'. If the becalmed suburbs of Belfast, with their washing lines and white linen, represent a society that seemed in 1965 (when 'Glengormley' was written) to have outgrown its own violent past, that past nevertheless haunts the edges of the poem in cryptic references to 'The unreconciled, in their metaphysical pain' who 'Dangle from lamp posts in the dawn rain'. Such deaths, it appears, are the price paid for the chance to live in 'A worldly time, under this worldly sky', the weary repetition of 'worldly' reinforcing the mood of acquiescence in a de-mythologised 'new era'. As Hugh Haughton observes: 'the whole poem is another reluctant statement of belonging'. We might also note that Mahon's suburban sky, unlike the sky above Molloy's head, is entirely empty of birds.

Before we leave *Night-Crossing* we should look briefly at a poem which sets out, in a very deliberate, artistically conscious way, Mahon's stall as a poet. 'Carrowdore' is subtitled 'at the grave of Louis MacNeice' and was written after Mahon, Longley and Heaney had visited the churchyard on the Ards peninsula where MacNeice is buried. The three poets resolved to write an elegy for their Northern Irish predecessor, yet it was clear when Mahon later read his poem in Longley's flat that further poems on the subject would not be needed. Not only was it an exemplary memorial to MacNeice but also a definitive statement of literary allegiance. In 'Carrowdore' Mahon discretely positions himself in relation to the poet whose own conflicted identity as both an Irish and English writer Mahon has explored in essays and reviews. In 'MacNeice in Ireland and England', for example, Mahon quotes MacNeice's exasperated impatience with Ireland – 'Your drums and your dolled-up Virgins and your ignorant dead!' ('Valediction') – before going on to remark:

> There is a belief ... that Irish poetry, to be Irish, must somehow express the National Aspirations; and

MacNeice's failure to do so (the National Aspirations, after all, include patriotic graft and pious baloney) is one of the reasons for his final exclusion from the charmed circle, known and feared the world over, of Irish poets.

It is easy to see why Mahon found a kindred poetic spirit in the truculent Ulsterman. Yet there were other, more lyrical notes to be heard in MacNeice's verse – flashes of childhood memories or a sudden sensuous response to light and landscape. These qualities find their way into Mahon's homage to MacNeice – for example, in the delicate symbolism of 'the ironical, loving crush of roses against snow' where the juxtaposition of 'ironical' and 'loving' suggests 'that combination of romantic nihilism and idealism' which Sean O'Brien has identified as the distinguishing feature of Mahon's poetry. There is a further moment of self-identification when, conflating MacNeice, Homer and the blind Irish poet Raftery, the London of the Blitz with the trenches of the First World War (and in an eerily prescient way with Belfast), Mahon affirms the role of the poet as a harbinger of renewal:

> From the pneumonia of the ditch, from the ague
> Of the blind poet and the bombed town you bring
> The all-clear to the empty holes of spring,
> Rinsing the choked mud, keeping the colours new.

The silence that followed Mahon's reading of 'Carrowdore' was broken only by the sound of paper being crumpled as Heaney and Longley conceded defeat. It was an impressively mature performance for a young poet, and marked the emergence of a distinctive new voice in Irish poetry.

2

Lives (1972)

T HE YEARS BETWEEN 1968 AND 1972, when
Mahon's second book *Lives* was published, were both
personally significant – he moved to London, married and
embarked on a career as a freelance literary journalist –
and also politically momentous for the province. The fragile
calm of 'Glengormley' had given way to an intensification
of old hatreds that reached a climax in Bloody Sunday,
and it is against this background of violence that many of
the poems in *Lives* are set. The gods and heroes of Irish
legend may have been consigned to 'the histories' in *Night-
Crossing*, yet in Mahon's second collection there is a pained
awareness of the long shadows cast by religion, in particular
by the Ulster Protestantism in which he had been nominally
raised. Whereas in 'Spring in Belfast' the poet had, in a
characteristic sleight of hand, kept 'my own' at arms' length,
identifying and not identifying with those who would 'keep

sullen silence in light and shade,/Rehearsing our astute
salvations under/The cold gaze of a sanctimonious God',
in *Lives* the pathology of religious belief – or one form of it
– is more intensely felt. In 'Ecclesiastes' Mahon launches a
spittle-flecked satire on those who represent the rigidities
of sectarian faith:

> God, you could grow to love it, God-fearing, God-
> chosen purist little puritan that,
> for all your wiles and smiles, you are ...

The life-denying gloom of a typical Belfast Sunday is
caught in the evocation of 'dank churches, the empty
streets,/the shipyard silence, the tied-up swings', the last
image in particular suggestive of a profound psycho-sexual
repression. Such faith is seen as a negation, a refusal of the
world in all its vitality and contradictions. The speaker turns
upon the object of his satire in a complex manoeuvre that
implicates him in the same judgmental Calvinism of which
he accuses the Ian Paisley figure, on whom the poem could
easily be based. He urges himself to 'Bury that red/bandana
and stick, that banjo' in an attempt to kill off the wandering
troubadour poet and replace aesthetics with the exercise
of spiritual and temporal power: 'this is your/country, close
one eye and be king./Your people await you, their heavy
washing/flaps for you in the housing estates –/a credulous
people.' The poem ends with an ironic appeal to the black-
cloth clergyman whose moral denunciations have been
evoked in the poem's pulpit-thumping ventriloquism:

>   God, you could do it, God
>   help you, stand on a corner stiff
>   with rhetoric, promising nothing under the sun.

It is instructive to read this poem in the light of an essay by Tom Paulin published in the *London Review of Books* in 1982. In 'Paisley's Progress' Paulin attempts to define the nature of the Protestant fundamentalism that Mahon excoriates in 'Ecclesiastes':

> Paisley's particular kind of puritan egotism is voracious in its subjectivity and for all its insistence on sincerity is in practice highly theatrical. He is a compulsive role-player and is fond of dressing up in other people's personalities.

Paulin's character sketch clearly fits the rabble-rousing preacher of Mahon's poem: the same hectoring monomania, the strident self-assertion, the inflated rhetoric, all combine to create a powerful study in religious intransigence. Yet it is also a political intransigence, as Paulin and Mahon understand only too well, both poets being products of a culture that takes seriously the New Testament exhortation to 'come out from among them and be ye separate'. It could be argued that Mahon's poetic self-fashioning as an uncompromising aesthete is a secular channelling of a religious impulse towards separatism, a resistance to, and suspicion of, mainstream culture that at the same time belies an envious attraction to it. As Paulin notes in reference to Paisley's writings:

The plain, strenuous autodidactic atmosphere that clings to [his] published works ... tells of a disadvantaged population which feeds its persecution complex by reading the Psalms and which dreams of emerging from the underground status of subculture into the light of power and society.

Certainly there is a continuing tension in much of Mahon's poetry between a world-weariness, a *contemptus mundi*, and a more affirmative response to life. The challenge in reading Mahon is to work out where in each poem the fault-line between the two positions lies. In 'Ecclesiastes' the sheer venom of attack masks an anxious fear of being absorbed into the subculture it portrays, of sinking into a profound isolation. The title itself is a reminder that, according to that bleakest of all scriptural texts, 'all is vanity', and there is perhaps something in Mahon's temperament that answers to a need to negate, to gainsay. The result is a dramatic foreshortening of that 'humane perspective' found in the churchyard at Carrowdore and anticipates other poems in *Lives* which, in their more pared-down execution, enact a poetics of reduction, a search for a form and an idiom adequate to the harder edges both of contemporary Irish history and of Mahon's own sensibility.

In 'An Image from Beckett', for example, we see for the first time the deployment of a stripped-down verse form in place of the more expansive stanzaic patterns of previous poems. The use of unrhymed tercets, clipped lines and a curt, laconic voice is particularly effective in suggesting a mind on the edge, trying desperately to get some kind of purchase on its drastically reduced circumstances. Taking its cue from a line by Pozzo in *Waiting for Godot* – 'They give birth astride of a grave, the light gleams an instant, then it's night once more' – the poem moves through a series of snapshots, brief glimpses of a world seen from an open grave as the 'hard boards' are temporarily lifted to accommodate the latest tenant:

> In that instant
> There was a sea, far off,
> As bright as lettuce,
>
> A northern landscape
> And a huddle
> Of houses along the shore.

In Mahon's appropriation of the disembodied voice there is perhaps something reminiscent of Hardy's grimly comic post-mortem poems, such as 'The Levelled Churchyard' or 'Channel Firing'. However, without the consolations of rhyme and regular metre, Mahon's poem is a darker inquiry into the extremities of perception as memories and precognitions mingle in a future perfect tense that spans the generations.

> They will have buried
> Our great-grandchildren, and theirs,
> Beside us by now

With a subliminal batsqueak
Of reflex lamentation.

Mahon also shares with Hardy a preoccupation with the
scale of things, with the way geological time effaces
individual existence, rendering it null and void in the
context of human history as a whole. The posthumous
speaker returns to its present site of ruination, noting with
detached irony how 'Our knuckle bones/Litter the rich
earth/Changing, second by second,/To civilizations.' The
recycling of old or dead material (a trope that finds an
equivalent in Mahon's constant revising of his own poems)
is played out in existential terms against the backdrop of
an everyday world that, in a witty reversal, 'haunts' the
dead speaker, and which prompts the valedictory
conclusion:

To whom in my will,

This, I have left my will.
I hope they have time,
And light enough, to read it.

The content of the will is the poem itself, which in turn
becomes a bequest, a gift to the future from a troubled
present. 'An Image from Beckett' is one of many examples
of Mahon's attraction to the 'existential lyric', a form that
in its obliquity and terseness allows him to shine a brief
light into the surrounding darkness of modernity.

To do so, however, requires a radical displacement of the self, a rejection of the 'egotistical sublime' in an attempt to speak from centres of consciousness other than one's own. In 'Lives', for example, Mahon extends the range of voices possible in a poem to include those of a Celtic 'torc of gold', an oar 'stuck in the shore/To mark the place of a grave', 'a bump of clay/In a Navaho rug', a stone from Tibet and 'A tongue of bark/At the heart of Africa/Growing darker and darker'. These artefacts are not randomly chosen but offer a miniaturised autobiography of the planet itself, allowing the otherwise 'mute phenomena' to tell their own story in ways that, as Hugh Haughton puts it, 'blend the mythopoeic and the materialistic'. The 'I' of the poem splinters into a series of cultural memories, ranging backwards and forwards, from the Bronze Age to World War II and into the future. In the process the human is marginalised and the world of objects re-enchanted in a celebration of 'stuff' that will sound an increasingly dominant note in Mahon's poetry. The poem also continues the exploration of recycled lives that we saw in 'An Image from Beckett', although here it is not so much the litter of knucklebones that troubles the speaker as the detritus of memory itself: 'It all seems/A little unreal now'. The word 'now' is then repeated in the next line as the poem, emptied of sacred objects, brings into sharp, satirical focus the technological, military and economic presumptions of the present:

Now that I am

An anthropologist
With my own
Credit card, dictaphone,

Army-surplus boots
And a whole boatload
Of photographic equipment.

The awkward self-consciousness of these lines, their consonantal clutter and clatter, are in marked contrast to the sing-song, childlike tones that lift the earlier parts of the poem: 'That was fun ... The time that I liked/Best ... ' Now, in place of spontaneity and expressiveness, the speaker's language is functional, a mere listing of the accessories, the gadgets, that somehow seem to define him. In so doing the anthropologist becomes the object of his own investigations, a curiosity, almost a freak, someone so trapped in his own historical present, in the moment, that no real continuity across the centuries is possible:

I know too much
To be anything any more;
And if in the distant

Future someone
Thinks he has once been me
As I am today,

Let him revise

His insolent ontology
Or teach himself to pray.

Before we move on to examine what is arguably the finest poem in the collection – 'Beyond Howth Head' – we need to look briefly at a poem that presents a powerfully rebarbative account of what being trapped in the moment feels like when that moment is 1972, the year of Bloody Sunday. 'Rage for Order', without specifying a Northern Ireland context, evokes a recognisable sense of place with its reference to 'The scorched gable end/And the burnt-out/Buses'. Against this backdrop of violence (or rather 'somewhere beyond' it) we are told that 'there is a poet indulging his/Wretched rage for order – '. The phrase suggests Wallace Stevens's great poem, 'The Idea of Order at Key West', but there are crucial differences between the two poems and poets. Mahon reconfigures Stevens's '*blessed rage for order*' within a world of rioting and broken glass, where the kind of fastidious aesthetic implied in Stevens's poem is viewed as 'a dying art,/An eddy of semantic scruple/In an unstructurable sea.' Such high-mindedness is seen as an indulgence, an irrelevance, an art that is nothing compared to the claims of blood. Mahon's deracinated poet is 'far/From his people' and in that distance his poetry shrivels into empty gestures and a facile rhetoric. The poem offers little encouragement to the contemporary Northern Irish poet – to Mahon himself, exiled in England – unless we find it in the 'terminal ironies' of the artist whose reluctant loyalty compels him to simultaneously 'tear down/To build up'. A pall of smoke hangs over the poem as the city (Belfast, yes, but Dresden and Hiroshima too) burns on. The poet, however, can still 'make history' rather than be made by it, if only by countering political rage with poetry's rage for order, by fighting one sort of fire with another.

The scene shifts – and with it the tone – in Mahon's masterpiece of a verse letter, 'Beyond Howth Head'. Instead of the Belfast poet agonising in his London flat over his home town, we have the Dublin poet writing in a rather breezy style (appropriately, considering the invocation of the wind at the beginning) to a friend in London. The mask of impersonality drops in favour of something more intimate and relaxed, notwithstanding the considerable formal control exercised throughout its eighteen eight-line stanzas. It is an excellent example of the way in which, as Seamus Deane has observed, 'the formal control ... is an expression of a kind of moral stoicism, a mark of endurance under pressure'. The use of rhyming couplets and the poem's tetrameter pulse combine to establish a light framework in which serious matters can be discussed. Here are the first few lines:

> The wind that blows these words to you
> bangs nightly off the black-and-blue
> Atlantic, hammering in its haste
> dark doors of the declining west
> whose rock-built houses year by year

collapse, whose children disappear
(no homespun cottage industries'
embroidered cloths will patch up these

lost townlands on the crumbling shores
of Europe); shivers the dim stars
in rainwater, and spins a single
garage sign behind the shingle.

With a few brief pencil-strokes, the poem sketches a coastline that, for all its local specificity ('from Carraroe to Dublin Bay') allows the poet to move in increasingly wider circles of literary allusion. The poem rarely settles for long on any one historical or cultural moment before it is carried, as on a wind of association, to another, giving the verse a rapid, impressionistic feel. The wind itself suggests not only the 'haystack-and roof–levelling wind/Bred on the Atlantic' of Yeats's poem 'A Prayer for my Daughter' but also the West Wind of Shelley's Ode, the *pneuma* of Romantic inspiration, and behind that the Holy Spirit, the breath of God. Yet as so often in Mahon's poetry the pressure of the past – whether in the form of Ireland's colonial history, Celtic myth, Christian symbolism or Greek and Chinese poetry – are brought into provocative relationships with the present. Collapsing houses, disappearing children, lost townlands – this is the reality of modern Ireland in the throes of diaspora and decay. The decline is terminal, the poem says, and any appeal to some redemptive myth of art, to the 'embroidered cloths' of a Yeatsian aesthetic, is in vain, no matter how much one may wish for them. The desolate image of a garage sign spinning in the wind is part of a whole matrix of 'signs' that point to an entropic sense of ultimate ruination.

However, as precarious as 'the rock-built houses', the poem is perched somewhere between despair and a willed, desperate hope. Against a soundtrack of American music the 'young girls coming from a dance' briefly illuminate the Dublin night. They are seen as 'lightning rods', conductors of sexual energy in a rigid, repressive society, reaching out to a modernity represented by pop music and English television. To borrow a phrase from Yeats's 'Sailing to Byzantium' (and Yeats is rarely far from the surface of 'Beyond Howth Head') the poem enacts a confrontation between the 'old men' and the 'young in one another's arms':

> What can the elders say to this?
> The young must kiss and then must kiss
> and so by this declension fall
> to scrawl the writing on the wall.
> A little learning in a parked
> Volkswagen torches down the dark
> and soon disperses tired belief
> with an empiric *joie de vivre.*

Here, within the context of a country in decline, urban graffiti blends into Hebrew prophecy while English satire – Pope's 'a little learning is a dangerous thing' – translates into teenage sex in a German car. The dark is temporarily ignited in a blaze of sensuality, as pleasure circumvents religious authority and finds expression in a French phrase. Mahon even makes a political connection between the young making love in Volkswagens and the 'lewde libertie' of Irish nationalists who, in 1598, 'torched' the house in Kilcolman owned by the poet Edmund Spenser, apologist for Elizabethan hegemony and enforcer of Tudor policies in Ulster. Sex and political struggle are here entangled, and the poet's own plea to those 'Ulster chieftains [who] looked to Spain' to 'come and inspire us once again' makes an additional link between pleasure, politics and the living breath of poetry. Writing thus becomes an act of resistance to repression, an example of what Mahon describes as the 'love-play of the ironic conscience'. To this end the poem summons the ghosts of other writers who have, by ironising metaphysical certainties, enlarged the sphere of human experience: Yeats, Milton, a Greek poet in the 'unquiet Cyclades', Beckett, the Japanese poet Chomei and Thoreau, whose rejection of materialism finds an echo in Mahon's ironic self-portrait as someone who, in another life perhaps,

> might exchange,
> since 'we are changed by what we change',
> my forkful of the general mess
> for hazelnuts and watercress
> like one of those old hermits who,
> less virtuous than some, withdrew
> from the world circles people make
> to a small island in a lake.

The lines incorporate a bewildering complex of allusion, from the Latin tag 'tempora mutantur, nos et mutamur in illis' (the precise Latin form of which the young Stephen Dedalus is quizzed about in Joyce's *A Portrait of the Artist as a Young Man*), through the Biblical story of Esau selling his birthright for a 'mess of pottage', to Christian monks on their island in Dublin Bay. The classical conception of time and time's exchanges, an Old Testament story about spiritual impoverishment, the witness of Catholic monasticism, and a modernist novel about an artist trying to 'forge the conscience of his race' are stitched together in a way that combines differently coloured imaginative threads, yet always with the same purpose: to find models of resistance to the 'general mess' of modernity. That 'mess' is differentiated into the random objects deposited by the tide as Mahon, deploying a characteristic trope, presents in list form the 'wild/eviscerations of the troubled/waters between us and North Wales/where Lycid's ghost for ever sails'. The reference to Milton's elegy to his drowned friend Edward King in *Lycidas* is almost thrown away as the poet surveys what the waves have thrown up:

> seaweed, wrack,
> industrial bile, a boot from Blackpool,
> contraceptives deftly tied
> with best regards from Merseyside

One almost expects the body of King himself to roll over gently in the surf.

This mingling of diverse phenomena – from the aesthetic products of high culture to the waste products of modern society – has a destabilising effect on the verse, creating a sense of shifting and fragmentary perspectives. The poem is full of images of shattering, of violent blows, whether it is the wind 'hammering' at the door, the shaking radio sets, Yeats's hill-men who 'still break stone', the Celtic saint Kemoc ringing the bell 'to crack the fourth-dimensional/ world picture of a vanished aeon', the 'plastic bombs' of Belfast or the American B-52s, whose 'grisly aim [is]/to render the whole earth the same'. The grisly pun in the word 'render' only reinforces the sense of an ending – and a rending – that pervades this poem of stark, hallucinatory violence.

Yet for all the apocalyptic storms that threaten to batter the poet into accepting 'Beckett's bleak reductio', the poem also records intermittent lighting effects, from the 'flash' of 'an *aisling*, through the dawn' to the moment when

> Spring lights the country; from a thousand
> dusty corners, house by house,
> from under beds and vacuum cleaners,
> empty Calor Gas containers,
> bread bins, car seats, crates of stout,
> the first flies cry to be let out,
> to cruise a kitchen, find a door
> and die clean in the open air

These Irish flies, released into a brief but 'clean' new life, not only participate in a fitful illumination similar to that provided by the Baily Lighthouse 'wink[ing] beyond Howth Head' in the final stanza, but also prefigure those other prisoners of darkness, the mushrooms that 'crowd to a keyhole' in Mahon's most famous poem 'A Disused Shed in Co Wexford'. This poem is the culmination of Mahon's third book of poetry, *The Snow Party*, and to this collection we shall now turn.

3

The Snow Party (1975)

THE SNOW PARTY CONSOLIDATED MAHON'S growing reputation as a poet of loss, abandonment and silence. The word 'lost' tolls through the collection like a muffled bell: in the evocation of a 'heaven/Of lost futures' in 'Leaves'; in the portrait of his sea captain father-in-law, the 'lost voyager' who 'lost [his] balance like Li Po' in 'A Curious Ghost'; in the glimpse in 'Nostalgias' of 'a lost tribe' singing 'Abide with Me' in 'a tiny stone church/On a desolate headland'; in the rescuing of 'a lost hubcap' in 'The Mute Phenomena', a discarded fragment of modernity in which 'is conceived/The ideal society which will replace our own.' This last point is particularly significant and provides the intellectual underpinning of the collection. By animating the inanimate world of turnips, cutlery, a brick wall and other 'mute phenomena' Mahon establishes a self-cancelling

point-of-view from which to observe the vanity of human
wishes. As he wryly notes:

> Be strong if you must, your brisk hegemony
> Means fuck-all to the somnolent sunflower
> Or the extinct volcano.

This leads to a radically different 'theology of things', a
re-scaling of the relationship between the individual and
the world. If 'God is alive and lives under a stone' then
where does that leave us? What survives of our self-image
as creatures made, allegedly, in the image of God? In 'The
Apotheosis of Tins' – a poem inexplicably omitted from
the *New Collected Poems* – the phenomena, the abandoned
'tins' of consumer culture, are no longer mute but highly
articulate forms whose language mimics the language of
the society from which they have been excluded. There is
an almost comic impersonation of a certain kind of
pedantic, donnish idiom as the tins wake to the
consciousness of their exilic state among the other rejects
on the sea shore:

> Deprived of use, we are safe now
> from the historical nightmare
> and may give our attention at last
> to things of the spirit,
> noticing for example the consanguinity
> of sand and stone, how they are thicker than water.

The use of Latinate vocabulary like 'consanguinity' may

be seen as a deliberate attempt to seize the linguistic high ground, to reclaim the 'things of the spirit' – a particularly suggestive oxymoron – by relocating human discourse in the context of rubbish. A form of anti-materialistic materialism, if you like. The second stanza continues the theme:

> This is the terminal democracy of hatbox and crab,
> of wine and Windolene; it is always rush-hour.

In a world where the 'rush-hour' – the constant movement of the tides – is almost entirely devoid of human presences, only the shadow of a pensioner on the beach briefly interrupts the process of self-definition before it too is summarily dismissed, together with 'your patronage, your reflective leisure'. In the final stanza the tins achieve their apotheosis (a word that carries within it the very idea of divinity) as 'promoted artefacts by the dereliction of our creator'. There is a delicate ambiguity in the way the word 'dereliction' points both to the things discarded and to the human creator whose dereliction of duty has laid waste the natural world. In a prophetic tone that sounds more like a threat, the tins anticipate their own futures as 'imperishable by-products of the perishable will', a permanent non-biodegradable reproach to humanity. In a daring act of textual appropriation, the tins reposition themselves at the centre of western literary culture, lying 'like skulls in the hands/of soliloquists', man-made *memento mori* for the next generation of Hamlets. Such objects will become the objects of veneration, secular and sacred, their last homes the science museum, their 'saintly devotion/to the notion/of permanence in the flux of sensation/and crisis' a matter for profound meditation, as on a Grecian urn.

Mahon's imagination is both haunted and clarified by the prospect of a world with little or no sense of *temenos*, or sacred space. In 'The Banished Gods' he redraws the map of nature to exclude the human, allowing the gods to hide, to 'sit out the centuries/In stone, water/And the hearts of trees,/Lost in a reverie of their own natures'. In this 'lost' world silence both deepens and intensifies sounds, birds sing 'with a noise like paper tearing' and 'the seas sigh to themselves/Reliving the days before the days of sail'. Significantly, the moor 'seethes in silence' only 'where the wires end', where human technology runs out. It is a place of preservation but also a place for mourning, a place that 'shelters the hawk and hears/In dreams the forlorn cries of lost species'. That word 'lost' again.

The homelessness of the gods, however, is fundamentally a human displacement, a banishment of the imagination to the margins of a society in thrall to 'zero-growth economics and seasonal change'. If Mahon's vision of

> a world without cars, computers
> Or nuclear skies,
> Where thought is a fondling of stones
> And wisdom a five-minute silence at moonrise

makes him sound like a 1960s radical, a counter-cultural critic of what used to be called 'the military-industrial complex', then that is because, at heart, he is. Born in 1941 (the same year as Bob Dylan) Mahon was a student at a time when many young intellectuals would naturally adopt an oppositional stance to the iniquities of consumer-capitalism. In one of the poems included in *The Yellow Book* (a volume we will look at more closely later) he describes Dublin in the sixties as

> golden days
> of folk revival, tin whistle and *bodhran*,
> ecology, yin and yang, CND, late-century blues,
> *Gandalf's Garden*, *Bananas* and *Peace News*.

It should come as no surprise, then, to find in *The Snow Party* poems that not only state but also enact their resistance to those 'mind-forged manacles' of materialism witnessed in an earlier age by Blake. In 'The Mayo Tao', for example, the speaker assumes the voice and persona of a Taoist hermit, a kind of oriental Thoreau transplanted to the Irish coast. The poem begins, appropriately, with an act of renunciation:

> I have abandoned the dream kitchens for a low fire
> and a prescriptive literature of the spirit

The phrase 'dream kitchens' cleverly catches both the sales-speak of modern advertising and also suggests the phantasmagorical nature of consumer desires. The poem proceeds to wrap the speaker in a Wordsworthian cloak of 'snow-lit silence', punctuated by the snores of the sea, 'conversation/with deer and blackbirds' and 'the sob story/ of a stone in the road'. Freed from human society, the speaker becomes

> an expert on frost crystals
> and the silence of crickets, a confidant
> of the stinking shore, the stars in the mud

The silence of the crickets is matched by the silence of the poet whose non-dualistic apprehension of the immanence in things drives him 'almost to the point of speech'. The poem ends, wittily, with a four-line stanza about writing a four-line poem about 'the life of a leaf'. We are told that he has been working on it 'for years' and that 'it might come out right this winter'. The joke could almost be called postmodern if it wasn't so Zen-like.

The eastern sensibility that infuses 'The Mayo Tao' is also everywhere present in the title poem of *The Snow Party*. The haiku-like tercets have the same kind of delicate sound patterning as 'a tinkling of china/And tea into china' while the snow that falls outside the window falls with an exquisitely modulated softness:

> Snow is falling on Nagoya
> And further south
> On the tiles of Kyoto;

Eastward, beyond Irago,
It is falling
Like leaves on the cold sea.

The cool transparency of these lines makes them resistant to empirical analysis, creating a distance between poet and reader that reminds us of the distinction made by Gerard Manley Hopkins, in a letter to Robert Bridges, between 'bidding' and 'monumentality' in poetry. 'Bidding' is the term Hopkins uses for 'the art or virtue of saying everything right *to* or *at* the reader ... and of discarding everything that does not bid, does not tell. It is most difficult to combine this bidding, such a fugitive thing, with a monumental style'. In 'The Snow Party' the monumental style predominates as the repeated use of present tense forms seeks to lift the poem out of historical contingency and into the wholly aesthetic realm of the tea ceremony. And yet, the poem implies, there is no such thing as a wholly aesthetic realm undisturbed by time. The poet Basho's visit to the snow party in 1688 coincided, on the historical plane, with atrocities 'elsewhere':

Elsewhere they are burning
Witches and heretics
In the boiling squares,

Thousands have died since dawn
In the service
Of barbarous kings;

The Battle of the Boyne, the Salem witch trials, Bloody Sunday: just some of the possible referents in these stanzas, half-buried allusions to real-time violence that undermine the contemplative detachment that pervades the rest of the poem. The poise returns, however, in the final stanza as the snow effectively silences political discourse in favour of aesthetic repose:

> But there is silence
> In the houses of Nagoya
> And the hills of Ise.

This dialectic between historical flux and the Keatsian stillness, or monumentality, of the achieved work of art is at the very centre of Mahon's work and provides the stimulus for one of the most internally conflicted poems of the collection: 'The Last of the Fire Kings'. Here, in this poem about responsibility and abdication, tribalism and the claims of art, Mahon rehearses, though more obliquely, many of the themes of Heaney's *North*, also published in 1975. The speaker, modelled on the anthropological figure of the priest-king as described in Sir James Frazer's *The Golden Bough*, longs to be released – through suicide if necessary – from 'the barbarous cycle' in which he has been immolated for the past five years. The poem records, in the same defamiliarising stanzaic form used in 'The Snow Party', a fantasy of escape:

I want to be
Like the man who descends
At two milk churns

With a bulging
String bag and vanishes
Where the lane turns,

Or the man
Who drops at night
From a moving train

And strikes out over the fields
Where fireflies glow,
Not knowing a word of the language.

This flight into silence is a flight from 'a world of/Sirens, bin-lids/And bricked-up windows', from 'the fire-loving/ People and the 'ancient curse' of history. Once again we see how deftly Mahon splices the contemporary with the mythic, superimposing an a-historical matrix onto an all-too historical situation. The result is not only a clash of cultural signs but a destabilising mingling of registers as the casual demotic of 'Either way, I am/Through with history' merges into an almost Yeatsian idiom as the fire-king perfects his

> cold dream
Of a place out of time,
A palace of porcelain

Where the frugivorous
Inheritors recline
In their rich fabrics
Far from the sea.

In a sense this is a reversal of the 'poetics of elsewhere'
explored in 'The Snow Party', as the 'elsewhere' in 'The
Last of the Fire Kings' is precisely that cold aesthetic figured
by the falling snow in the poem about Basho. As set out in
New Collected Poems the two poems face each other on
the page, two panels of a diptych, each holding up a frosted
mirror to its times.

The idea of 'a place out of time' brings us inevitably to
what has become Mahon's most celebrated exploration of
the poetics of elsewhere: 'A Disused Shed in Co Wexford'.
Mahon himself has lately sought to distance himself from
this signature poem, calling it 'a rather manufactured piece
of work'. Nevertheless, the poem has, rightly or wrongly,
acquired the status of a modern classic, 'the best single poem
written in Ireland since the death of Yeats', according to
John Banville. Its appeal is not difficult to understand: here
is a poem that creates a vivid sense of lives lost, victims not
only of human atrocities and natural disasters but of that
historical amnesia, that indifference to suffering, which
Auden captured in 'Musée des Beaux Arts', where 'the
splash, the forsaken cry' of the falling Icarus goes
unremarked. Auden's awareness of the heartlessness at the
heart of civilization, of the way tragedy takes place 'While
someone else is eating or opening a window or just walking

dully along' is matched by Mahon's acute ear for voices off, for the sounds of a world going about its business only a short distance away from unimagined horrors:

> Spiders have spun, flies dusted to mildew
> And once a day, perhaps, they have heard something –
> A trickle of masonry, a shout from the blue
> Or a lorry changing gear at the end of the lane.

The 'they' in question are the 'thousand mushrooms' that 'crowd to a keyhole' in the disused shed of the title, who 'have been waiting ... in a foetor/Of vegetable sweat since civil war days', in whose abandonment the reader is asked to find an analogue for the plight of those whom Frantz Fanon named 'the wretched of the earth'. This, then, is the central conceit of the poem: a comparison between the 'feverish forms' of multiplying fungi (is there a weak pun in the word 'mushroom', a suggestion of claustrophobia, of having no 'room', not even the 'elbow room' or *lebensraum* demanded by those nearest the door?) and the fate of history's unrecorded, unlamented dead. This is certainly a bold – though not entirely original – trope. J.G. Farrell's 1961 novel *The Lung* which Mahon had read – has its central polio-afflicted character say: 'I'm a pale fungus growing towards the light'. This is followed by a description of a disused potting-shed full of 'long, sickly white shoots racing each other interminably across the earth floor towards the minute bead of light from the keyhole.' Mahon's version of this scene creates some truly disturbing, science fiction moments, from 'the pale flesh flaking/Into the earth that nourished it' to the startling, caught-on-camera vision of these 'Powdery prisoners of the old regime,/Web-throated, stalked like triffids, racked by drought/And insomnia'. The phrase 'the old regime' reminds us that history is, indeed, a nightmare for those who cannot escape from it.

And yet. The poem's allegory invites us to suspend disbelief, to find a fitting emblem for adversity in the fate of some long-forgotten mushrooms. The pathetic fallacy at work here requires the mushrooms to display human characteristics that push the poem almost to the edge of comedy. They 'crowd' and have 'desire', they have 'learnt patience and silence/Listening to the rooks', they are 'groaning for their deliverance' and 'begging us ... to do something, to speak on their behalf'. By the end of the poem they have mutated into the 'lost people of Treblinka and Pompeii' with a plea for deliverance and a message for the future: 'Let not our naïve labours have been in vain'. The problem with allegory, however, is that it always runs the risk of snagging on some inconvenient fact. In the case of this particular parable the premise is undermined by one crucial objection, namely that there is nothing that mushrooms like more than dark, damp places like disused sheds. Not only would they wish to remain in such a hospitable environment, they would presumably resent (if such a word is permissible) any attempts to deliver them from it by well-meaning, liberally minded mycologists. Or poets.

Arguably, the poem suffers from being in two minds about itself, or perhaps there are two different poems fighting, like the fungi in the shed, for breathing space. The first is the one outlined above, the political allegory, the poem of historical engagement, with its allusions not only to Nazi concentration camps and volcanic rain, but Bastile prisoners, Hiroshima ('the world waltzing in its bowl of cloud') executions and the Irish civil war. The debt the poem owes to the latter as a framing device is well known. The dedication to J.G. Farrell – author not just of *The Lung* but also *Troubles*, a novel set during the Anglo-Irish war of 1919 and featuring a burnt-out hotel in Co Wexford – alerts us to a contemporary interpretation of the poem as a commentary on the Troubles of 1975. This was the year that saw the publication of Heaney's *North*, and Heaney himself has chosen to locate Mahon's poem exclusively in a Northern Irish context:

> Mahon, the poet of metropolitan allusion, of ironical and cultivated manners, is being shadowed by his unlived life among the familiar shades of Belfast. Do not turn your back on us, do not disdain our graceless stifled destiny, keep faith with your origins, do not desert, speak for us: the mushrooms are the voices of belonging but they could not have been heard so compellingly if Mahon had not vacated the whispering gallery of absence not just by moving out of Ireland but by evolving out of solidarity into irony and compassion. And, needless to say, into solitude.

Coming from the author of such locally sourced, Ulster-rooted poems as 'Funeral Rites' and 'Punishment', this could almost be read as a veiled reproach to his fellow Irishman for being, to quote John Hewitt once more, 'an airy internationalist', detached from his roots. Heaney seems to want the poem to witness to the specific crisis in the 'North', but as Hugh Haughton observes: 'To anchor the poem in the North of Ireland is to rob it of its own mobility on behalf of the immobilized'. The poem is clearly a larger work than Heaney allows.

There is, however, another way of looking at 'A Disused Shed in Co Wexford' and that is to see it as a poem concerned not so much with historical perspectives as with spatial ones. After all, the title directs us to the shed itself, and not to what is inside it. In a recent essay, 'Huts and Sheds', published in *Selected Prose* (2012), Mahon has explored at some length the semiotics of enclosed spaces. He begins, autobiographically, by recalling the ready-made structures of his childhood: the customs huts on the North-South border, the post-war Belfast prefabs, site offices, nightwatchmen's shelters on waste ground, school bicycle sheds, wooden annexes, changing rooms, caddie shacks, phone boxes. He mourns the imminent demolition of a local Golf Club pavilion to make way for new housing, remembering with affection the clubhouses of his teens, and describing in detail the adjacent huts and sheds that provided 'living quarters' for hardware of all kinds. 'These places,' says Mahon, 'these tiny palaces, were kept locked and were the more mysterious in that condition'.

The elision of 'places' and 'palaces' looks back to the Fire King's 'cold dream/Of a place out of time,/A palace of porcelain'. The contents may differ according to culture but the act of looking in, the 'glimpse' itself, even if only in dream, is seen as 'privileged', especially when the enclosed space is 'your old-fashioned hermetic box unknown to the catalogues'. The word 'hermetic' confers on the physical entity an almost metaphysical significance, suggesting an annexing of space that makes reflection possible, the creation of a place where 'a thought might grow'.

In language that owes something to Gaston Bachelard's *The Poetics of Space* – a seminal text in Mahon's understanding of interiors – the rest of the essay goes on to consider, among other things, the difference between a hut and a shed ('a hut you could live in, a shed not'), their shared character as 'sites of reverie' immune to market forces, and the prominence of both in the spiritual and intellectual history of humanity, from the hut where Odysseus finds shelter, through their repeated representation in art, to Heidegger's 'thinking hut' in the Black Forest. Mahon reminds us that 'Christ was born in a shed', that Lady Chatterley has sex in one and that Dylan Thomas wrote poetry in 'a humble shed nesting high above the estuary' at Laugharne. As Mahon says: 'Interesting things happen in huts and sheds', notably those thoughts – 'disgraceful thoughts, metaphysical thoughts, revolutionary thoughts' – that grow in 'primordial huts of the mind, in shady sheds of imagination'. It is here, where inner and outer meet, that the doors that provide the interface ('the precarious safety of the edge') between the self and the world open or close. Mahon goes on to argue that 'historically we preferred a closed cosmos, one with walls and a starred ceiling', and that 'the imagination rests in structure, containment'. The essay ends with a paean to solitude and an image that recalls that disused shed in County Wexford: 'The riches of this world will be found in a handful of dust or the faint stir of a cobweb'.

4

Poems 1962-1978 (1979)

THAT MAHON CHOSE TO LIVE OUT his creative
life in 'the precarious safety of the edge' may be seen
in the way he refused the security of a permanent 'base' in
the seven years between *The Snow Party* (1975) and his
next collection *The Hunt by Night* (1982). After a spell in
London, followed by two years in rural Surrey, Mahon and
his family returned to Northern Ireland in 1977 on his
appointment as writer-in-residence at the University of
Ulster at Coleraine. This return to the North, to the site
labelled 'home', should have offered an opportunity to
explore the complexities of his own disfigured culture, yet
it proved a difficult, indeed desperate, experience as he
struggled to establish the sort of connection with place and
people that Heaney, for example, continued to articulate.
Mahon's preference for urbanity over provincialism,
together with the personal crisis of mental and marital

breakdown, conspired to make his time on the North coast particularly fraught. Little was published in the two years he spent in Coleraine, and looking back in a later essay – 'The Coleraine Triangle' – he casts a sardonic, almost Larkinesque eye over the place, with its 'strange combination of derivative hedonism and sabbatarian grimness' and concludes that even if it is not the place's fault, there is something about the inhabitants of the place – from the uniformed, homophobic thugs to the middle-aged women in bungalows 'full of photographs and possessions but few books, and those few by Somerset Maugham' – that makes it *un beau pays mal habité*.

The phrase had already been used by Mahon in 'The Sea in Winter', one of the three major poems that did come out of this period – 'Going Home' and 'Autobiographies' being the other two. All three poems (which were published in the 1979 retrospective collection *Poems 1962-1978*) may be seen as attempts to cast, if not a cold eye over 'home', a notably cool one nevertheless. Their flatness of tone and detached gaze betray an attitude that could easily be mistaken for disdain – they are, as Hugh Haughton puts it, 'a study in not being Seamus Heaney' – were it not for the attention Mahon gives to those moments when the grey, rain-lashed landscape of the North is suddenly back-lit by a dramatic image or a vivid memory. In 'Going Home', for example, Mahon bids a prolonged farewell to the English pastoral life he had experienced in Surrey before turning to face the bleaker prospect of Northern Ireland.

> I am taking leave of the trees,
> The beech, the cedar, the elm,
> The mild woods of these parts
> Misted with car exhaust
> And sawdust, and the last
> Gasps of the poisoned nymphs.

This leave-taking turns not only on notions of farewell but also of de-naturing. With its nod to *The Waste Land* and its faint echo of Hopkins's 'Goldengrove unleaving' in 'Spring and Fall', Mahon's poem enacts a narrative of withdrawal that combines Spenserian allegory with intimations of ecological death. Central to the first five stanzas is a sense of the speaker as an incongruous figure, a belated observer of the English scene, whose clumsy attempts at blending in with his surroundings only confirm his status as at best an outsider, at worst a harbinger of destruction, flicking ash into the rose bushes 'as if I owned the place'. That provisional 'as if' is crucial to the poem's exploration of place and no-place. It is repeated in the first line of the next stanza – 'As if the trees responded/To my ignorant admiration' – before the speaker indulges in a fantasy of rootedness as he imagines himself turning into a tree 'like somebody in Ovid'. He develops the conceit to allow for an almost Heaney-style metamorphosis as the poet becomes

> a home for birds,
> A shelter for the nymphs,
> [Gazing] out over the downs

As if I belonged here too.

The dream of belonging evaporates with the third and final 'as if' of the poem, as if all such dreams of belonging are merely exercises in evasion.

What cannot be evaded, however, are the claims made on the imagination by the very place which should, as Mahon had acknowledged in 'Spring in Belfast', 'engage more than my casual interest,/Exact more interest than my casual pity'. As if to atone for his former disengagement, Mahon returns in the second half of 'Going Home' to an Ulster landscape where trees are 'few and far between'. This is a poem about absence, about what is not there, a poem that follows a kind of *via negativa* in order to arrive by a process of elimination at some emblem of endurance:

> Out there you would look in vain
> For a rose-bush; but find,
> Rooted in stony ground,
> A last stubborn growth
> Battered by constant rain
> And twisted by the sea wind
>
> With nothing to recommend it
> But its harsh tenacity
> Between the blinding windows
> And the forests of the sea,
> As if its very existence
> Were a reason to continue.

Significantly, the tree is stripped even of its identity as a tree, reduced to a mere 'growth', the word punning painfully on its double sense of the organic and the pathological. The sound patterning of the lines is also important: the 'st' in 'stony' is picked up in 'last', 'constant', 'twisted', 'forests' and 'existence', the awkwardness of the consonantal blend contrasting starkly with the softer acoustic effects of 'winking woodlands' and 'rose-bush'. It is hard not to hear the word 'resistance' under the surface of the text, for the tree seems to exist only to resist the wind and the rain. In this sense the tree becomes paradigmatic of Mahon's reluctant identification with the isolationist mentality of Ulster Protestantism, an ambivalent return to a 'home' without the attendant comforts suggested by the word. Indeed, the penultimate stanza sees the poet pushing the concept of belonging to its very edge:

> Crone, crow, scarecrow,
> Its worn fingers scrabbling
> At a torn sky, it stands
> On the edge of everything
> Like a burnt-out angel
> Raising petitionary hands.

In a reverse of the earlier metamorphosis from man to tree, the tree now mutates first to a barely human form, then to a bird of ill-omen, before finally reducing to inanimate object. This time it is the hard 'c' and 'sc' sounds that dominate ('crone', 'crow', 'scarecrow', 'scrabbling', 'sky') as if to mimic the scratching of the tree's gnarled, arthritic fingers. In an astonishing image of urban and spiritual devastation Mahon invites us to see the tree as the charred remains of a brittle culture, one in urgent need of absolution and renewal. The 'burnt-out angel' stands as a reproof and a warning, an image of Belfast certainly, but also of Mahon himself, burnt-out as a poet and with no direction home other than to the margins of the imagination. The final stanza extends the self-portrait:

> Grotesque by day, at twilight
> An almost tragic figure
> Of anguish and despair,
> It merges into the funeral
> Cloud-continent of night
> As if it belongs there.

The poet's final placement is in the darkness of death itself, yet even that provides no sense of place, only a speculative – 'as if' – temporary lodging.

It is perhaps with some relief that we turn from the 'bleak *reductio*' of 'Going Home' to the less anguished but still ambiguous world of 'Autobiographies', a poem that recalls another disenchanted revisiting of place: Larkin's 'I Remember, I Remember'. In that poem the speaker, staring out of a train window at a barely recognised home town, responds to the question 'Was that where you had your roots?' with 'No, only where my childhood was unspent ... just where I started.' The poem proceeds to summon a

whole series of imagined youthful scenarios only to dismiss
the exercise as an elaborate fiction, a chronicle of events
and relationships that never happened. The poem
concludes with the wry observation that 'Nothing, like
something, happens anywhere'.

A similar amnesia threatens to immobilise the
imagination at the beginning of the first part of
'Autobiographies', a section significantly sub-titled 'The
Home Front'. The first two stanzas describe what the young
Mahon, born two years into the Second World War, did
not see: the siege of Leningrad, bombs falling on Belfast,
searchlights illuminating the sky. A lexis of numbness and
containment – frozen armies, a child's cot, the black-out –
suggests a repudiation of sensory experience, a regulation
and darkening of vision. Light is 'metered', while sleeping
under the *stairs* makes looking up at the *stars* impossible.
Images, graven or otherwise, are denied the child, already
absorbed into a Protestant renunciation of the world.
However, just at the point where darkness threatens to
occlude the past completely, the poem opens out to the
world as early recollections break the surface of
consciousness. The child is 'held up to the window', but
also to history as 'soldiers, sailors and airmen' parade before
his eyes and a post-war childhood begins. The poem
acquires a degree of facticity as it lists, in a typical Mahon
procedure, the accumulated contents of memory. These
include:

The last ration coupons,
Oranges and bananas,
Slick sidecaps and badges
And packets of Lucky Strike.

Gracie Fields on the radio!
Americans in the art-deco
Teashops! The released Jews
Blinking in shocked sunlight ...
A male child in a garden
Clutching the *Empire News.*

The poem pans out from the debris left behind in a Belfast air-raid shelter to a more global legacy as the caesura separating 'teashops' from 'the released Jews' brings into disturbing focus the realities of war. The transferred epithet in 'shocked sunlight' destabilises the poem's orderly catalogue of memories and forces the reader to make a subliminal connection between the Holocaust and the poet, now recast in the third person as a precocious reader of '*Empire News*'. The choice of newspaper, the description of him as a '*male* child' and his placement in a garden bring together, in a complex relationship, notions of imperial aggression, masculinity and original sin. In a few lines the poem has shifted from autobiography to history, from private memory to public discourse, as the young Mahon, clutching his newspaper, reads his way into the world.

That world takes an increasingly sensuous, if not erotic, form in the next two sections of the poem. In 'The Lost Girls' Mahon moves swiftly from a gendered identification with war-time heroics – running around the playground 'pretending to be a plane' – to a more feminised sensibility as he follows 'at a respectful distance' the teacher's daughter, Eileen Boyd. The distance then shortens as from his window he watches her – 'a white dress picking flowers' – in her back garden. The girl comes in and out of focus as details of her biography – the large house, her future life with an older man in Kenya, the names of friends – are sublimated into something more like myth as 'her light, graceful figure/ Luminous and remote' joins hands with the other 'lost girls in a ring/On a shadowy school playground'. In a gesture towards Botticelli's *Primavera*, the final image of the section preserves the lost girls in an aesthetic gaze, transforming them into 'nymphs dancing together/In a forgotten spring'. In allegorising a moment in history the poem restores to memory what had been forgotten, returning the poet to his source, to the 'spring' of creativity where the 'nymphs' – no longer poisoned or absent as in 'Going Home' – can continue their dance.

However, in the third section, 'The Last Resort', the mood has become significantly more downbeat. A thin film of depression settles over the poet's memories of family seaside holidays, turning the title into a bleak pun. The poem is unsparing in its photo-realist montage of 'salad-and-sand sandwiches/And dead gulls on the beach', while 'Arcadia', the ironically named ice-cream parlour, provides only a shelter from the driving rain. A pervasive sense of ennui, exacerbated by 'Dull days in the harbour,/Sunday

mornings in church', is momentarily lifted in the second
stanza by a vision of the hotel maid climbing the stairs, a
glimpse of stocking that sends the young Mahon to his
room in a state of heightened sexual awareness. This erotic
interlude ends suddenly, however, as the poem jumps
forward in time to paint a gloomy picture of a place that
has since sunk even further into obscurity:

> Years later, the same dim
> Resort has grown dimmer
> As if some centrifugal
> Force, summer by summer,
> Has moved it ever farther
> Towards a far horizon.

That move towards the horizon, towards marginality,
is the same 'centrifugal force' that drove the burnt-out
angel-tree to 'the edge of everything' in 'Going Home'.
As we have seen, 'centrifugal' is an apt word to
characterise Mahon's preference for circumference over
centre, yet that preference is complicated by an anxious
awareness that the condition of exile may all too easily
turn into a vapid, moneyed detachment as the *nouveaux
riches* exchange the Ulster coast for the sands of Tenerife,
'far from the unrelaxing/Scenes of sectarian strife'. The
poem rejects this kind of 'airy internationalism', seeing
in it a failure of nerve, a flabby, sun-tanned
irresponsibility. (The word 'unrelaxing' is particularly
well chosen.) Instead, the poem remains unfashionably

loyal to somewhere whose reality continues to impinge
on the imagination:

> Yet the place really existed
> And still can crack a smile
> Should a sunbeam pick out
> Your grimy plastic cup
> And consecrate your vile
> Bun with its parting light.

For all its shabbiness, there is also a fleeting numinosity
about the place. The word 'consecrate' illuminates the final
stanza and in so doing temporarily redeems all that is
cracked, grimy, plastic or vile.

In the fourth and last section, 'The Bicycle', the mood
changes yet again as emotion is recollected in excitement.
In a subtle recycling of Wordsworth's famous line 'There
was a boy ... ' the poem foregrounds the bicycle itself, giving
it human agency in a further attempt at de-centering:

> There was a bicycle, a fine
> Raleigh with five gears
> And racing handlebars.
> It stood at the front door
> Begging to be mounted;
> The frame shone in the sun.

The boy identifies so closely with the bike that he loses
all sense of separateness from it, or from the landscape
through which he speeds. He becomes 'half/Human, half
bike', a hybrid creature whose days are spent in a blur of

'dips and ridges', his dreams full of 'valves, pumps, sprockets,/Reflectors and repair kits'. The bike takes him not only out of himself but out of the North, following 'rough and exotic roads' into a Republic that is both geographical and metaphorical. The bike is his entry to a wider world, and also acts as an emblem of poetry itself. Though he eventually sells it in Dublin we are told that:

> its wheels still sing
> In the memory, stars that turn
> About an eternal centre,
> The bright spokes glittering.

The imagery of wheels, stars and spokes brings together a constellation of ideas that are rarely far from the surface of Mahon's poetry, preoccupied as it is with the relationship between home – the 'eternal centre' – and the exilic imagination, represented by the spinning, singing wheels. The stars that the child failed to see at the start of this sequence are now visible through the telescope of poetry, and this faith in the efficacy of art is maintained, albeit precariously, in a creative tension between centrifugal and centripetal forces. The two forces here balance each other at last, centre and circumference now connected by those 'bright spokes glittering'.

Such moments, however, are often negated, or at least threatened, by a lowering of spirits, a mood swing towards a deadening of response that in other poets would be disastrous. Mahon, however, shares with Larkin a dolefulness that often becomes, paradoxically, the default setting for some of his best work. 'Deprivation,' said Larkin famously, 'is for me what daffodils were to Wordsworth'. For Mahon 'deprivation' is another word for a profound sense of physical and metaphysical foreshortening, an awareness that just as a pier is – in the words of Stephen Dedalus – a disappointed bridge, so a bungalow might be said to be a disappointed house. It is from just such a flattened perspective – 'a draughty bungalow in Portstewart' – that the poet looks up at the night sky above him in 'The Sea in Winter', the one truly great poem that came out of Mahon's residency in Coleraine. Like 'Beyond Howth Head', the poem is cast in the form of a verse letter, this time addressed to friend and fellow-poet, Desmond O'Grady. That earlier poem had ended with the speaker preparing for bed as he 'put[s] out the light/on shadows of the encroaching night', but now the insomniac poet roams restlessly after dark making unfavourable comparisons between the '*beau pays mal habité*' of the Northern Irish coast and the 'white island in the south' where he and O'Grady had shared a Greek holiday. A longing to be elsewhere than 'Up here where the air is thinner' involves the poet in a complex bi-location of the self in which what is imagined acquires a reality absent from what is merely observed:

> beside my 'distant northern sea',
> I imagine a moon of Asia Minor

> bright on your nightly industry.
> Sometimes, rounding the cliff top
> at dusk, under the convent wall,
> and finding the little town lit up
> as if for some island festival,
> I pretend not to be here at all

The imagined full moon shining down on his friend as he writes is the source of a creativity denied the speaker, for whom Portstewart is illuminated only *as if* for play and pleasure. (Note the proximity of the convent wall). In fact, we are told in the next stanza that the light that 'blinds the foam/and shingle' is the artificial fluorescence coming from the shops along the front. Yet by pretending to be absent from the scene, Mahon performs a kind of double-take, seeing the strip-lighting as 'the dancing lights/of Naousa', the frosty pavements of the town as 'the pavements of that distant star' and the 'cold, glistening sea mist' as the Northern equivalent of a Mediterranean spume. This to-ing and fro-ing between opposed geographies is replicated on an acoustic level too. The long open vowel sound in the word 'nights' in the first line of the poem establishes a pattern for the rest of the stanza:

> Desmond, what of the blue nights,
> the ultramarines and violets
> of your white island in the south,
> 'far-shining star of dark-blue Earth',
> and the boat-lights in the tiny port
> where we drank so much retsina?

In contrast the short 'i' sound is frequently deployed to suggest constriction and a narrowing of perspective, an emotional thinning out in keeping with the 'thinner' air of the North. This is particularly noticeable in the description of 'the little town lit up/as if for some island festival' where the long 'i' in 'island' (a word that surely belongs to the imagined elsewhere) is conspicuous among the diminished sounds that surround it. We might also observe the way 'lit' is incorporated in 'little' as if to emphasise the town's meagre quality of light and life.

If the first three stanzas have a dreamlike, *chiaroscuro* quality to them, the return to waking consciousness in the next three is described with a flatness of tone that matches the grey hung-over skies of the morning. The poetic imagination 'scatters', along with the 'relics of last night's gale-force wind', the word 'relics' combining a sense of shoreline detritus with an ironised longing for whatever remnants of religious experience may be found. An air of defeated energy hangs over the verse:

> far out, the Atlantic faintly breaks,
> seaweed exhales among the rocks
> and fretfully the spent winds fan
> the cenotaph and the lifeboat mine;

Against this backdrop of exhausted possibilities – the slant rhymes are particularly effective in conveying this incompleteness – the only sign of life is in the form of the door-to-door Ormo van that 'delivers, while the stars decline.' Yet what the grocery van 'delivers' are perishable goods, food for the outer, not the inner man. In this wasteland of the spirit – 'policed by rednecks in dark cloth/and roving gangs of tartan youth' – the poet (to whom we sense 'The Sea in Winter' is implicitly addressed) feels profoundly alienated: 'No place for a gentleman like you'. Desperate to find some saving grace to set against the entropic rhythms of the stars – 'there *is* that Hebridean sunset' – Mahon wryly acknowledges that 'a strange poetry of decay/charms the condemned hotels by day', a fully rhymed couplet that could almost stand as a summary of Mahon's work as a whole. Yet the phrase 'poetry of decay' can be read in two senses: a poetry that delineates decay or a poetry that is itself in a decayed state. Both readings are necessary if we are to get a sense of the cultural pessimism that threatens to overwhelm the poem.

This pessimism extends in the seventh stanza to a self-denigrating picture of the poet as a marginal figure, experiencing 'the delirious sense/of working on the circumference'. The language becomes, briefly, hieratic with its Yeatsian gesture to 'the midnight oil' and 'elusive dawn epiphany', before succumbing to the doubt (or 'faith' as he puts it – the two words are hard to pull apart) that 'the trivia doodled here/will bear their fruit sometime, somewhere'. The use of a comic-sounding word like 'doodled' circumvents any possibilty of Romantic self-inflation while the vagueness of 'sometime, somewhere' casts doubt on the poet's hope that 'the long winter months may bring/gifts to the goddess in the spring'. The subliminal allusion to Sweeney and Mrs Porter in these lines adds to our sense of the unlikelihood of any goddess stepping forward to receive a poet's 'gifts'. Moreover, nature herself seems implacably opposed to the aesthetic gaze, as we see in the first two lines of the next stanza:

> The sea in winter, where she walks,
> vents its displeasure on the rocks.

The alliterative, iambic, consciously 'poetic' first line – is there a nod to Byron's 'She walks in beauty'? – gives way to the trochaic violence of the second line and in the process loses the personification of the sea as a female figure, replacing 'she' with 'its', turning the sea into something bad-tempered and punitive. The image of the sea breaking on the rocks leads almost by a train of association to the sea-embattled fortress of Hamlet's Elsinore:

> The something rotten in the state
> infects the innocent; the spite
> mankind has brought to this infernal
> backwater destroys the soul;
> it sneaks into the daily life,
> sunders the husband from the wife.

An undercurrent of sexual conflict – the key word is 'displeasure' – can be felt in this stanza, the impersonality of 'the husband' and 'the wife' universalising the tragic drama that was being played out in Mahon's private life as he faced the prospect of his own 'rotten' marriage.

As if to rescue himself from his sorrows, Mahon once again reaches out to a universe of 'things', steadying himself – as Wordsworth once steadied himself against a wall to confirm the objective world – in an attempt to heal the breach between subject and object. Whether it is 'the rattle/ of a cat knocking over a milk-bottle/on a distant doorstep by moonlight' or 'the weird/facticity of this strange seaboard', the poet welcomes the intrusion of the ordinary and contingent into the myth-making world of the imagination. The everyday rubs up against the ideal as the poem performs a dizzying high-wire act of 'heroism and cowardice', an inevitable consequence of living 'on the edge of space'. A chastened resolve not to 'ever again contemptuously/refuse [the] plight' of his own Ulster history, but to 'find the narrow road to the deep/north the road to Damascus' alternates with something more enabling as language itself undergoes a kind of conversion experience. The penultimate stanza enacts a poetics of transcendence, each image of wholeness contributing to a teleology of secular redemption:

> One day, the day each one conceives –
> the day the Dying Gaul revives,
> the day the girl among the trees
> strides through our wrecked technologies,
> the stones speak out, the rainbow ends,
> the wine goes round among the friends,

> the lost are found, the parted lovers
> lie at peace between the covers.

But this is a projection, an anticipated closure in the manner of Shakespearian comedy: 'But Jack shall have Jill/ Naught shall go ill'. Typically, Mahon ends *The Sea in Winter* on a note of self-denial, foregoing the pleasures of Romance for the 'displeasure' of quotidian existence:

> Meanwhile the given life goes on;
> there is nothing new under the sun.

In figuratively donning the black-suited cloth of the Preacher, with his purse-lipped denunciations of human vanity, Mahon reveals (perhaps more than intended) a latent, suppressed self-identification with the 'God-fearing, God-/chosen purist little puritan' that he had satirised in 'Ecclesiastes'. Certainly the last stanza returns us to the mundane, to a world where 'dogs bark and the caravan/ glides mildly by'. Yet even at this low imaginative ebb, the poem is poised precariously between negation and affirmation. The phrase 'the given life' may be interpreted more generously than we had first allowed, while the image of the caravan gestures simultaneously to the suburban and the exotic. There is surely some promise of new life in the thought that 'if the dawn/that wakes us now should also find us/cured of our ancient colour-blindness ... ' even if the ellipsis allows the thought to trail off as grey skies fill up the canvas. The poem concludes with a wry self-portrait, reminding us of Mahon's creative difficulties during this period. The irony of a non-writing writer is not lost on Mahon:

> I who know nothing go to teach
> while a new day crawls up the beach.

The monosyllables of the last line convey a weariness of mind as the poet figuratively drags himself out of the sea of unconsciousness. And yet there is perhaps a final ambivalence here: the nothingness which the poet experiences is felt at the same time ('while') as the 'new day', the words 'know' and 'new' standing on either side of 'nothing' as if the dissolution of the self is at the very heart of all true knowledge and renewal.

5

The Hunt by Night (1982)

FOR MAHON THAT RENEWAL CAME IN the form of a welcome relocation to London in 1979 and a pamphlet of poems published in 1981 called *Courtyards in Delft*, a collection that prefigured his next major publication *The Hunt by Night* in 1982. Many of the poems in *Courtyards in Delft* re-emerge in the later volume and so it is *The Hunt by Night* that we shall look at now as representing Mahon's increasingly engaged and wide-ranging exploration of what might be called 'the poetics of elsewhere'. Three poems in particular – 'North Wind', 'Rathlin' and 'Derry Morning' – revisit familiar terrain in that they deal with the historical and aesthetic fall-out from 'the Northern Ireland situation', yet seen through the longer lens of exile in England. It is as if, before moving outwards into new imaginative spaces, Mahon had to circle back once again to the troubled sites of personal and historical memory. In 'The Sea in Winter' Mahon had exhorted himself to 'never forget the weird/facticity of this strange seaboard' and in 'North Wind' that pledge is made good in the first two stanzas:

> I shall never forget the wind
> On this benighted coast.
> It works itself into the mind
> Like the high keen of a lost
> Lear-spirit in agony
> Condemned for eternity
>
> To wander cliff and cove
> Without comfort, without love.
> It whistles off the stars
> And the existential, stark
> Face of the cosmic dark.
> We crouch to roaring fires.

However, just as the sea, glimpsed in the following day's sunlight, is 'scarred but at peace', so the poem, unlike 'The Sea in Winter', seems more reconciled to itself, more accepting of 'the lit town where we live', more forgiving of 'The wrapped-up bourgeoisie/Hardened by wind and sea'. The poet refuses the opportunity to 'weigh anchor and leave', content to number himself among those 'dancing mad in the storm', seeing himself anthropologically through the eyes of bemused visitors.

> What did they think of us
> During their brief sojourn?

The 'us' is a significant indicator of identification with a world which, for all its political and cultural impoverishments offers a baptism of the imagination unavailable elsewhere:

> Everything swept so clean
> By tempest, wind and rain!
> Elated, you might believe
> That this was the first day –

The language merges the idiom of the Bible with traditional Protestant values of good housekeeping and cleanliness, even if 'chaos and old night' are never very far away. The poem may be read as a valorisation of all that is meant by 'here' and a corresponding repudiation of that 'elsewhere' which Mahon wittily depicts as an artificial paradise curated by Edouard Manet and William Burroughs:

> Elsewhere the olive grove,
> Naked lunch on the grass,
> Poppies and parasols,
> Blue skies and mythic love.
> Here only the stricken souls
> No springtime can release.

Thought – however painful – is preferred to a Keatsian life of sensation, while faith is privileged over the aesthetic gaze in a reversal of terms that further underlines Mahon's conflicted sense of himself as a 'recovering Ulster Protestant from Co Down'. The final stanza tips the balance decisively away from humanist ideas of self-empowerment – 'the subtler arts' – towards something more abject and compelling:

> Prospero and his people never
> Came to these stormy parts;
> Few do who have the choice.
> Yet, blasting the subtler arts,
> That weird, plaintive voice
> Sings now and forever.

It is difficult not to add an 'Amen' to the final line as its phrasing owes much to the language of prayer and hymn. Indeed, Mahon has acknowledged the formative influence of the hymns that he sang as a Church of Ireland choir boy, not only in terms of sensibility but also as paradigms of a certain kind of rhyming stanzaic patterning. 'The hymnology invaded the mind,' he has said in an interview, and on a formal and substantive level 'North Wind' brilliantly exploits the resources of that hymnology to merge the 'high keen' of the wind with the 'plaintive' music of 'stricken souls'.

Wind music of an equally plaintive kind breathes through the poem 'Rathlin'. This records a trip to an island off the North Antrim coast that had been the site of a brutal attack in 1575 by an English fleet commanded by the Earl of Essex. During the massacre (in which over 500 people were slaughtered) the screams of the women could be heard on the mainland, borne 'on a north-east wind'. The first few lines of the poem telescope the distant past into a narrative of return as the natural noises of the island gradually colonise and fill the silence left by the murdered women:

> A long time since the last scream cut short –
> Then an unnatural silence; and then
> A natural silence, slowly broken
> By the shearwater, by the sporadic
> Conversation of crickets, the bleak
> Reminder of a metaphysical wind.

Modernity, in the form of an outboard motor, interrupts the 'dream-time' of nature as the boat delivers a party of tourists who land 'as if we were the first visitors here'. Like latter-day Darwins in the South Atlantic they find a world that in the absence of human agency has become a sanctuary for 'amazed/Oneiric species [that] whistle and chatter'. The poem records a 'Cerulean distance, an oceanic haze', the word 'distance' implying more than merely geographical separation. This is a site of memory in which memories have been effaced – the action of the birds in 'evacuating' the rock-face is significant – to be replaced by 'Nothing but sea-smoke to the ice-cap/And the odd somnolent freighter'. In the next line Mahon briefly switches attention back to the mainland, now seen from the perspective of the island, to set up a contemporary parallel to the violence of the past – 'Bombs doze in the housing estates' – before dismissing present realities in favour of symbolic truth:

> But here they are through with history –
> Custodians of a lone light which repeats
> One simple statement to the turbulent sea.

In these densely charged lines we catch in the lighthouse image an echo both of Milton's 'Il Penseroso' – 'Or let my lamp at midnight hour/Be seen in some high lonely tower' – and also Yeats's tower at Thoor Ballylee, from whose crumbling battlement he resolved to 'Fix every wandering thought upon/That quarter where all thought is done'. Mahon's complex dialogue with the English and Anglo-Irish poetic tradition is enacted in these allusive engagements, giving the poem an ambivalent sub-text. It also positions the poem as a reaffirmation of his own commitment to that aesthetic distance he had explored, and to some extent repudiated, in 'Rage for Order'. Indeed the language of that earlier poem – in particular the definition of poetry as 'An eddy of semantic scruple/In an unstructurable sea' – is strikingly similar to the lines quoted above, with the significant difference that the 'one simple statement' repeated by both lighthouse and solitary poet is here a validation of imaginative truth, battered as it is by the turbulent sea of history. However, the poem does not end on that consolatory, timeless note but rather pitches us back into time to find a voice for the victims of 'unspeakable violence'. In a subtle transference of language, the screams of the Rathlin women are blended into the 'cry of the shearwater/And the roar of the outboard motor' as the visitors prepare to leave the island and its 'singular peace' and re-enter history. Yet history itself is seen as profoundly problematic, reducing the poet to a spray-blindness that could be interpreted as tears. The poem ends with the poet questioning the idea of history as past, suggesting instead that the screams of the Rathlin women – what took place *here* – are being and will be repeated and heard again *elsewhere.*

> Spray-blind,
> We leave here the infancy of the race,
> Unsure among the pitching surfaces
> Whether the future lies before us or behind.

To turn from 'Rathlin' to 'Derry Morning' (the poems face each other in the *New Collected Poems*) is to be reminded of just what that *elsewhere* looks like when it has become the *here* of the present. Mahon's physical distance from the scene he describes – the poem was written in London – is in no sense a detachment but rather a necessary precondition for a more sustained engagement. London, of course, merges into Londonderry – a Unionist appropriation of place – which in Mahon's poem is returned to its original nomenclature, Derry, meaning an oak-grove. Exile thus enables the poet to see the place in its present aspect and what he sees he translates, albeit ironically, into the mythic world of the *aisling* tradition.

This is a form of poetry which personifies Ireland as a beautiful young girl who will lead the Nationalist cause in much the same way that the bare-breasted Liberty leads the French revolutionaries in Delacroix's famous painting. Yet the reality is painfully different:

> The mist clears and the cavities
> Glow black in the rubbled city's
> Broken mouth. An early crone,
> Muse of a fitful revolution
> Wasted by the fray, she sees
> Her *aisling* falter in the breeze,
> Her oak-grove vision hesitate
> By empty dock and city gate.

This is a city waking up to its own 'rubbled' present, an old hag exploring the cavities in her mouth left by yesterday's bombs. These are the bombs that 'doze in the housing estates' in 'Rathlin' and which have since been detonated. The poem records the after-shock of violence in terms of a stunned imagination as the idealistic dreams symbolised by the figure of the *aisling* 'falter'. 'Here' is a city overshadowed by helicopters, a place whose recent history is already fading in memory:

> Here it began, and here at last
> It fades into the finite past
> Or seems to: clattering shadows whop
> Mechanically over pub and shop.
> A strangely pastoral silence rules
> The shining roofs and murmuring schools.

The third stanza relives the city's violent past in a way that comes close to valorising it. The description of 'this tranquil place' as 'recently a boom-town wild/With expectation' is double-edged as the word 'boom-town' combines opposing images of vitality and destruction. Similarly, the 1968 civil rights march in Derry and the violence that followed are presented in language that shares some of the excitement it describes as 'each unscheduled/ Incident' becomes 'a measurable/Tremor on the Richter scale/Of world events, each vibrant scene/Translated to the drizzling screen'. The word 'drizzling' prepares us for the final stanza's grainy (and rainy) attempt at some sort of accommodation between past and present as the poet tries to make sense of the 'change envisioned here,/The quantum leap from fear to fire'. The blurring of the sound barriers between 'here' 'fear' and 'fire' corresponds to a similar blurring of memory caused by 'the returning rains/That shroud the bomb-sites, while the fog/Of time receives the ideologue'. The poem ends on a distinctly melancholic note with the image of 'A Russian freighter bound for home' as it 'Mourns to the city in its gloom'. The nationality of the freighter (in 'Rathlin' it was merely 'the odd somnolent freighter') is important as it provides a telling reminder of another revolution that failed. It also reminds us that, like the Russian freighter, Mahon too is 'bound for home' in all the rich ambiguity that the phrase suggests.

These three poems then – 'North Wind', 'Rathlin' and 'Derry Morning' – may be seen as necessary staging posts on the journey to a more inclusive, cosmopolitan poetry. They are, in a way, attempts to act out the resolution Mahon made in the very first poem that appears in the *New Collected Poems*, 'Spring in Belfast'. Back then, 'walking among my own', he had acknowledged that 'One part of my mind must learn to know its place'. The debt now paid, Mahon allows himself the freedom to explore the other part of his mind, the part that does *not* know its place, in poems that represent an 'elsewhere' to counterbalance the 'facticity' of 'here'. That 'elsewhere' is increasingly located for Mahon in art and artefact, as we see in one of the central poems of this period, 'Courtyards in Delft'.

'Courtyards in Delft' may be read on a number of different levels: as a poem about a particular painting (*The Coutyard of a House in Delft* by the 17th-century Dutch painter Pieter de Hooch); as a poem about Dutch domestic paintings in general; as a poem about the medium and texture of paint itself; as a meditation on art and its relations to the everyday; as an examination of the scope and limitations of realism; as an oblique commentary on Protestant attitudes to artistic representation; as a compressed history of Dutch colonialism; as a thinly-veiled critique of Northern Irish culture; as an exercise in autobiography. All of these strands are deftly woven into the fabric of the text and cannot be separated out, yet any account of the poem must start by focusing on the language used to replicate in words what Mahon had seen in the National Gallery.

The first line of the poem immediately establishes the terms of the discourse that follows:

Oblique light on the trite, on brick and tile –

The word 'trite' carries with it a value judgement, a reluctance to confer significance on the scene and on the objects that fill up the canvas. Yet as readers of Mahon's poetry we should by now be familiar with that revaluation of values that informs his work, his restoring of significance to what is commonly ignored, or even despised. As Bachelard says in *The Poetics of Space*:

> What a joy reading is, when we recognise the importance of these insignificant things, when we can add our own personal daydreams to the 'insignificant' recollections of the author! Then insignificance becomes the sign of extreme sensitivity to the intimate meanings that establish spiritual understanding between writer and reader.

Applying Bachelard's words to the painting, what is 'trite' is redeemed by the 'light' that touches it, the internal rhyme bringing together the humble and the illustrious in a way that hints at a secular transfiguration. The word 'oblique' also gestures towards a diffused spirituality, the angled nature of the light suggesting something close to the angel of the Annunciation in a Fra Angelico painting. In a sense, de Hooch's painting is – *mutatis mutandis* – a Dutch variation on an Italian theme with 'brick and tile' now included among the objects of grace. This is borne out in the epithet chosen to describe the built environment of the courtyard – 'Immaculate masonry' – where the appropriation of a word with theologically specific references to the Virgin Mary further complicates a painting that is, essentially, an idealisation of the Protestant work ethic. That ethic is rendered actual in the listing of objects selected for their usefulness in maintaining the link between cleanliness and godliness:

> and everywhere that
> Water tap, that broom and wooden pail
> To keep it so.

Up to this point painting and poem have merged in the sense that the same realism of representation has been applied in paint and language. The poet describes what the painter sees. However, a certain irony enters the poem at this point as an implicit parallel is made between the lives of the women in the painting and the domestic routine of women in the Belfast suburbs familiar to Mahon:

> House-proud, the wives
> Of artisans pursue their thrifty lives
> Among scrubbed yards, modest but adequate.
> Foliage is sparse, and clings; no breeze
> Ruffles the trim composure of those trees.

The adjectives are faintly damning: 'thrifty', 'scrubbed', 'modest', 'adequate', 'sparse', 'trim'. This is an indictment of a culture in six words, and one that we have seen before in earlier poems. The word 'trim' in particular sends us back to 'Glengormley', with its lowering depiction of a society that 'has tamed the terrier, trimmed the hedge/And grasped the principle of the watering can'. The distance between that watering can and the wooden pail in the painting is minimal. Furthermore, the absence of a corresponding breeze in the Dutch courtyard is symptomatic of an artistic lack, a failure of imagination, the 'composure' of the trees a poor substitute for composing.

The diminished world of the courtyard is further explored in the second stanza with its negative accumulation of things that are not there:

> No spinet-playing emblematic of
> The harmonies and disharmonies of love,
> No lewd fish, no fruit, no wide-eyed bird
> About to fly its cage while a virgin
> Listens to her seducer

Here there is no 'sensual music' for the righteous soul to be caught in; the painting has achieved a kind of stasis by its exclusion of anything – particularly sex – that might disturb the surface calm. Both poem and painting enact an emptying-out of instinctual life, of all that 'mars the chaste/ Perfection of the thing and the thing made.' The painting also enacts its own immaculate conception in the consciously gendered way it presents the courtyard as an enclosed feminised space, the only male intrusion being the gaze of the painter. The woman and the girl who inhabit the yard and whose eyes are fixed on each other are part of the 'chaste/Perfection' of the painting, a painting complete with its own Madonna and (female) child.

Yet to read the word 'chaste' in a wholly negative sense is to fail to respond to the nuances of tone that make this poem so finely balanced. After all, we have the evidence of poems like 'A Portrait of the Artist' to suggest that Mahon, like Yeats, was deeply drawn to the ideal of aesthetic detachment from 'whatever is begotten, born and dies', and, like the poet of 'The Tower', sought 'such a form as Grecian goldsmiths make/Of hammered gold and gold enamelling'. Van Gogh's journey south in 'A Portrait of the Artist' is an attempt to find the place where art and religion meet, to find a common source for each in 'A meteor of golden light/On chairs, faces, and old boots'. If art is an ordering principle then that 'rage for order' is clearly manifest in 'Courtyards in Delft' where 'Nothing is random, nothing goes to waste.' This valorisation of orderliness is balanced against its opposite, an existential fear of the randomness and waste of 'nothing'.

Similarly, it is possible to view 'That girl with her back to us who waits/For her man to come home for his tea' from more than one perspective. In the painting she is framed within an arched corridor that opens out onto the sunlit street and there is a quality of absolute stillness about her that is both negatively and positively charged. She may well embody a female passivity, the buried life, the plight of women throughout history who have waited for 'her man' (surely we can hear an Ulster inflection in the phrase?) to give meaning to their lives. Yet she is also detached from history, a solitary woman with her back turned on the petty-bourgeois round of domestic duties, her waiting memorialised in paint. Unlike the other two female figures, she looks out rather than in, waiting 'till the paint disintegrates/And ruined dikes admit the esurient sea'. As constituted by that paint, her own destruction and the destruction of the painting she inhabits are one, giving her an archetypal status that sets her apart from the foregrounded quotidian world. The stanza ends, however, with a reaffirmation of the value of 'mute phenomena', a re-commitment to the object as artefact and to the poetics of space:

> Yet this is life too, and the cracked
> Outhouse door a verifiable fact
> As vividly mnemonic as the sunlit
> Railings that front the houses opposite.

As if to develop the idea of the 'verifiable fact', the last stanza attempts to situate the poet's own biography within the frame of the painting. Memory, however, is less amenable to verification than facts and the opening words – 'I lived there as a boy' – are simultaneously true and untrue. They are only true if one reads the 'there' as pointing to a congruence between the oppressive orderliness of the Dutch courtyard and the equally oppressive orderliness of the Protestant culture that Mahon grew up in. If that reading is correct, then we may accept that the poem has been, in part, a disguised autobiography all along, or at least an attempt, based on experience, to make sense of a culture in which art is treated with suspicion. Whichever way we read it, the ambiguities remain. As Hugh Haughton puts it: 'Does the sunlit courtyard represent a benign childhood epiphany mirrored in a Dutch painting, or a claustrophobically tidy place the poet needed to escape from into art? Is it a haven against violence and disorder, or shaped by it?' Certainly, the image of 'the coal/Glittering in its shed' suggests a life contained, a variation perhaps on the mushrooms crowding to a keyhole in that other more celebrated shed. Further images of light appear with the 'late-afternoon/Lambency informing the deal table,/The ceiling cradled in a radiant spoon'. The reflection of the ceiling in a spoon creates a distortion of scale common in childhood experiences, and the use of the word 'cradled' sets up the lines that follow:

> I must be lying low in a room there,
> A strange child with a taste for verse,
> While my hard-nosed companions dream of war
> On parched veldt and fields of rainswept gorse.

The self-portrait in the first two lines suggests the essentially secretive, fugitive nature of poetry ('lying low') in contrast to the 'hard-nosed' culture of violence in which that poetry is situated. The room is yet another instance of 'places where a thought might grow', a 'dream home' which provides an alternative to the 'dream of war' of the last two lines. That dream turns into the 'nightmare of history' from which the poet is trying to awake, a dream of Dutch colonialism and Northern Irish bloody-mindedness that threatens to destabilise the poem's commitment to the aesthetic ideal represented so tentatively in both painting and poem.

Such an ideal is, essentially, a static one and poems like 'Courtyards in Delft' have been criticised for, in the words of Peter McDonald, an 'irresponsible aestheticism that always looks the other way'. A more nuanced reading, however, might see such poems as an attempt to negotiate between the frozen stillness of a certain kind of art – what Patrick Kavanagh called 'the difficult art of not caring' – and an acquiescence in the ineluctable process of material decay. If, as Blake believed, 'Eternity is in love with the products of Time' then Mahon's reworking of that dialectic is a more melancholy affair. This dialectic (which owes much to Yeats as well as Blake) is also apparent in 'A Garage in Co Cork' where the lexis of decay threatens to undermine any more metaphysical affirmations. The garage is as disused as the shed in County Wexford and the silence that hangs over 'this quiet corner of Co Cork' is palpable. The poem invites us from the very beginning to 'pause', to rewind memory and summon up again

                              the mound
Of never-used cement, the curious faces,
The soft-drink ads and the uneven ground
Rainbowed with oily puddles, where a snail
Had scrawled its pearly, phosphorescent trail.

The verse moves with a slow, somnolent pace, the word
'scrawled' concealing the crawl of the snail in a way that
subtly conflates writing and nature. The trail left by both
snail and literature is, however, 'pearly' and
'phosphorescent', adjectives that acquire a nimbus of light
from their juxtaposition with the earthiness of cement, just
as the ground itself is transfigured by its relation to the
rainbow. This evocation of still life is exactly that: a
registering of stillness permeated by a life unseen by the
casual observer. The second stanza takes us further into
and behind the stillness to hear the faintest of pulses from
the past:

          Like a frontier store-front in an old western
          It might have nothing behind it but thin air,
          Building materials, fruit boxes, scrap iron,
          Dust-laden shrubs and coils of rusty wire,
          A cabbage white fluttering in the sodden
          Silence of an untended kitchen garden –

The details in these lines – alternating between material
facticity and something more elusive – convey a
shimmering sense of the interpenetration of substance and
spirit, of building materials and butterflies, thin air and

scrap metal. This secular theology has an eastern inflection: the nothingness behind the film-set façade of the garage may be likened to the 'emptiness' of phenomena as described in Buddhist philosophy, a hint made explicit in the appeal to 'Nirvana!' at the beginning of the next stanza. However, the longing for an escape from time into stillness is cut short by the irruption into the poem of all that daily life which the poem had sought to exclude. Like spectators in a cinema, we watch as the tableau of the past unfreezes and the 'characters' step out of stasis and back into their former lives:

> But the cracked panes reveal a dark
> Interior echoing with the cries of children.
> Here in this quiet corner of Co Cork
> A family ate, slept, and watched the rain
> Dance clean and cobalt the exhausted grit
> So that the mind shrank from the glare of it.

The poem is now animated, verbs taking on a more central role in the remembrance of lost time, in the recreation of a world seen through a glass darkly. The poem raises fundamental questions about the relationship between memory, place and time, and the role of poetry in restoring what has faded. In particular, the poem itself acts as a site of memory, locating an imagined home for those who have been exiled to the margins as a result of Irish emigration:

> Where did they go? South Boston? Cricklewood?

Somebody somewhere thinks of this as home,
Remembering the old pumps where they stood,
Antique now, squirting juice into a cream
Lagonda or a dung-caked tractor while
A cloud swam on a cloud-reflecting tile.

There is more than a hint of Wordsworthian self-consciousness in the image of the reflected cloud; indeed, the next stanza offers further instances of those 'spots of time' when memory and meaning converge to give to the everyday what M.H. Abrams calls a 'natural supernaturalism':

Surely a whitewashed suntrap at the back
Gave way to hens, wild thyme, and the first few
Shadowy yards of an overgrown cart track,
Tyres in the branches such as Noah knew –
Beyond, a swoop of mountain where you heard,
Disconsolate in the haze, a single blackbird.

Echoes of MacNeice's poem 'The Sunlight on the Garden' mingle with Biblical resonances; however, the debt to Wordsworth is implicit and the last two lines in particular seem to owe something to Wordsworth's great meditation on memory, 'The Solitary Reaper'. In this poem the presence of a maiden singing her 'plaintive numbers', her songs of 'natural sorrow, loss, or pain' has a consolatory effect not only on herself but on the poet who overhears her. The girl is carefully positioned as 'single in the field', the word 'single' suggesting not just solitariness but a kind of undivided, Zen-like concentration. This state of mind allows her song to transcend all other songs, including those of the nightingale and cuckoo, and ensures that as the poet 'mounted up the hill,/The music in my heart I bore,/Long after it was heard no more.' The materiality of song thus gives way to music in its permanent Platonic form, and what was merely 'heard' through the ears is now apprehended in the mind. In Mahon's poem it is the 'single blackbird' whose song is transmitted to an unidentified 'you', perhaps one of the children whose cries echo through the disused garage. However, the syntax is ambiguous: is it the 'you' or the blackbird which is 'disconsolate in the haze'? Or both perhaps?

Such a merging of human and bird would be in keeping with Mahon's commitment to a more holistic view of our place in nature and his increasing concern with ecological issues. The idea of obsolescence, in particular, begins to haunt the margins of his poetry with greater urgency as he explores the life-cycle of both organic and inorganic matter. In 'A Garage in Co Cork' he imagines the fate of all those material objects which he has so meticulously recreated – 'those old pumps' for example – and speculates on what will happen to them. The words 'antique' and 'antiquities' are deployed in a way that suggests an underlying anxiety about the perishability of forms:

> Left to itself, the functional will cast
> A deathbed glow of picturesque abandon.
> The intact antiquities of the recent past,

> Dropped from the retail catalogues, return
> To the materials that gave rise to them
> And shine with a late sacramental glow.

The cycle is carefully observed: what begins with a 'deathbed glow' falls into 'dropped', then incorporates a 'return' and a 'rise', before ending with another 'glow', only this time a sacramental one. The stanza enacts its own resurrection, its own deliverance from oblivion, the language itself a recycling of the sacred. Indeed, sacred myth interrupts the secular narrative of obsolescence in a wonderfully dramatic and witty way in the penultimate stanza where Mahon, in a procedure clearly modelled on Ovid's 'Metamorphoses', describes the intervention of divinity into the lives of the garage owners:

> A god who spent the night here once rewarded
> Natural courtesy with eternal life –
> Changing to petrol pumps, that they be spared
> For ever there, an old man and his wife.
> The virgin who escaped his dark design
> Sanctions the townland from her prickly shrine.

In the light of this modern day metamorphosis we now read the poem backwards, as it were, to see the petrol pumps for what they are as mythopoeic objects : transfigurations of the mundane, material world into something else, a manoeuvre that dignifies not only the old couple but the forms into which they have been changed. In this dual perspective, matter and spirit are one, albeit in a thoroughly pagan sense, as the reference to the shrine at the end reminds us. The final verse provides a fitting conclusion to this meditation on 'time past and time future' as the poet sees such wayside memorials as part of a wider imperative to bring the banished gods out of exile and into our local, earthly habitations:

> We might be anywhere but are in one place only,
> One of the milestones of Earth residence
> Unique in each particular, the thinly
> Peopled hinterland serenely tense –
> Not in the hope of a resplendent future
> But with a sure hope of its intrinsic nature.

That the gods of imaginative life have indeed been banished from modern culture is a theme that Mahon frequently returns to, as if his own sense of himself as an artist in exile requires repeated validation through the example of other poets who have lived on the margins. One of the key poems in *The Hunt by Night* is 'Ovid in Tomis', a witty and morose monologue in the voice of the banished poet Ovid, exiled from Rome by Augustus on account of his *Ars amatoria*, the poet's hymn to erotic love. Now, 'set down/On an alien shore' he contemplates his 'own transformation/Into a stone' as he surveys the detritus washed up on the shores of the Black Sea. In a brilliant collapsing of myth and historical time Mahon/Ovid wonders 'What coarse god/Was the gearbox in the rain/ Beside the road?', a question that sets up a train of speculative thought on the metaphysics of rubbish as well as establishing the poem as an elegy for absent divinities: 'What nereid the unsinkable/Coca-Cola/Knocking the icy rocks?'

The speaker invites us to share his sense of geographic and psychic dislocation in a tone that combines outrage, wounded pride and a melancholy acceptance of his own marginality. The conventions of dramatic monologue allow Mahon to maintain a certain ironic distance from the speaker, opening up multiple perspectives on the Ovidian poet (who is also an honest Ulsterman) in ways that remind the reader of Robert Browning. However, the identification across the centuries between the Irish and the Roman poet is clearly established as some of Mahon's own anxieties over modernity's mission creep are filtered through the reflections of the poet in exile:

> No doubt in time
> To come this huddle of
> Mud huts will be
>
> A handsome city,
> An important port,
> A popular resort
>
> With an oil pipeline,
> Smart terraces
> And even a dignified
>
> Statue of Ovid
> Gazing out to sea
> From the promenade.

It is hard not to see in this view of imperial economic progress an oblique commentary on modern Ireland and its late-capitalist accommodations. Even the statue of the poet is presented ironically as a token gesture towards a desired cultural capital to go with the technological and industrial hardware. But the gaze of the poet is resolutely turned away from such matters, settling instead on the birds that provide the speaker with a reminder of what is perennial: 'I often sit in the dunes/Listening hard/To the uninhibited//Virtuosity of a lark/Serenading the sun/And meditate upon/the cording/Of motor-car tyres.'

The word 'cording' puns on the loss of harmonic relations between man, nature and those deities which, as Blake reminds us, 'reside in the human breast': 'Pan is dead, and already/I feel an ancient/Unity leave the earth.'

The speaker laments the fact that 'The Muse is somewhere/Else, not here/by this frozen lake'. Yet the poem, paradoxically, incorporates a heightened lyrical awareness of a divinised nature, of those 'endless forms so beautiful' that Darwin memorably evokes in *The Origin of the Species.* Rejecting Pascal's terrifying vision of 'infinite spaces' the poet appeals to his implied listener to 'concentrate instead/ On the infinity/Under our very noses —//The cry at the heart/Of the artichoke,/The gaiety of atoms.'

The poem ends on a note of resistance — a characteristic Mahon response to the pressure of modernity — as he contemplates the cycle of change that has produced the blank piece of paper in front of him. In a radical reversal of the earlier process whereby Syrinx in her incarnation as a reed is fed into 'pulping machines', the material that transforms into paper has been 'woven of wood nymphs', the word 'of' setting up a syntactical ambiguity that allows the paper to be physically constituted from myth itself. This insight leads to a profound reverence for natural methods of production that omit human intervention altogether:

> Better to contemplate
> The blank page
> And leave it blank
>
> Than modify
> Its substance by
> So much as a pen-stroke.
>
> Woven of wood nymphs,
> It speaks volumes
> No one will ever write.

It is instructive to consider 'Ovid in Tomis' in the light of the 'Introduction' to Blake's *Songs of Innocence*, a poem that records a descent into materiality as the pipe played by the speaker at the command of the child is exchanged for a 'hollow reed' which is then 'made' into a pen which 'stained the water clear'. The staining of the water, the writing down of the song, coincides with the vanishing of the child, the vacating of divinity from the realm of human discourse. Something similar is enacted at the end of Mahon's poem as the poet, reading in the unwritten volumes of the wood nymphs the sufferings of nature, can only respond with a slight movement of the head, a gesture of prayer and resignation:

> I incline my head
> To its candour
> And weep for our exile.

'Courtyards in Delft', 'A Garage in Co Cork' and 'Ovid in Tomis' all share in their titles a sense of place and space, of local habitations that are either preserved in art, reclaimed by myth or reluctantly embraced by the exilic imagination. In all three poems Mahon maintains that characteristic tone of engaged detachment which gives to his poetry its intellectual grace and tact. Such tact is made literal at the beginning of 'The Globe in Carolina' – the last poem in *The Hunt by Night* and one which also adopts a syntax of relation in its title – through the physical action of spinning a globe:

> The earth spins to my fingertips and
> Pauses beneath my outstretched hand;

The pause at the end of the first line precisely enacts the motion of the globe as it 'pauses' at the beginning of the second, one of the poem's many delicate touches. Indeed, there is a delicate mediation in these lines between human agency and natural rhythm, between the life-size fingers of the speaker and the miniaturised earth. Any suggestion of dominance, of lording it over nature, is cancelled by the yearning hinted at in the gesture of the 'outstretched hand', a gesture that combines both longing and belonging. Although the poem establishes a distance between the poet and the globe as viewed from space, there is nothing imperious in the perspective. The earth may be beneath him but it is not beneath him. Rather, the poet's 'mild theoptic eye' allows him a vision of the earth as a moving, breathing organism with its own self-determining verbal energy:

> White water seethes against the green
> Capes where the continents begin.
> Warm breezes move the pines and stir
> The hot dust of the piedmont where
> Night glides inland from town to town.
> I love to see that sun go down.

Having set the world in motion in a way that comes close to parodying the Biblical narrative of creation, the poet removes himself from the scene as elemental forces of nature – water and wind – move and stir the earth into animation. There is even the faintest of allusions in the final line – 'I love to see that sun go down' – to the Creator-God of Genesis who looked at his work and *saw that it was good.* Such allusions are essentially ironic, though, for the poem makes no concession to any creationist account of human origins but insists, rather, on the existential miracle of there being anything at all. Indeed, from the human angle of the 'anglepoise' that 'rears like a moon to shed its savage/

Radiance on the desolate page' the earth is viewed in the context of those arts and natural sciences represented by 'Dvorak sleeves and Audubon/Bird-prints'. The reference to Dvorak is particularly apposite as not only does it bring together the Czech composer exiled in New York and the similarly estranged poet, home-sick in Carolina, but it also glances at the 'New World' both composer and poet are seeking to recreate in their respective mediums. The third stanza in particular offers a panoramic view of that part of the globe in which Mahon, as resident alien, is himself located, an interesting bifocal vision that telescopes distances and allows for the poet to be included in his own supreme fiction:

> From Hatteras to the Blue Ridge
> Night spreads like ink on the unhedged
> Tobacco fields and clucking lakes,
> Bringing the lights on in the rocks
> And swamps, the farms and motor courts,
> Substantial cities, kitsch resorts –
> Until, to the mild theoptic eye,
> America is its own night-sky.

As the lights go on in Carolina and the night sky becomes a constellation of resemblances (a trope that Mahon developed in four stanzas that were cut from the original version of the poem) so the poet adopts a Neil Armstrong-like position 'Out in the void and staring hard/At the dim stone where we were reared'. The word 'void' calls to mind Estragon's mordant observation in 'Waiting for Godot' that 'there's no lack of void' and also re-echoes the 'silence/Of the infinite spaces' heard by Ovid in his exile on the Black Sea. Notions of cosmic homelessness inform the poem, raising crucial questions regarding the relationship between us and the 'dim stone' we call planet earth. In the next few lines Mahon refuses the consolations of orthodox belief in favour of a kind of eco-feminism that restores the earth to her proper role as 'Great mother' or Gaia. His impassioned apostrophe to a feminised earth reads like a secular penitential prayer, an *Ave Maria* for our times.

> Great mother, now the gods have gone
> We place our faith in you alone,
> Inverting the procedures which
> Knelt us to things beyond our reach.
> Drop of the ocean, may your salt
> Astringency redeem our fault.

Mahon plays off the abstractions of religion – 'gods', 'faith', 'redeem', 'fault' – against the minute particular of a drop of ocean in an attempt not only to revaluate values but to attend to what he calls, in 'The Apotheosis of Tins', the 'things of the spirit'. The collocation might equally be reversed to allow us to speak of the 'spirit of things'. Either way, the materialism of Mahon's vision is tempered by a sense of the numen, and vice versa. Having said that, he is careful not to retreat into a specious spirituality. Against the charge that his ecological commitment is, like 19th-century Romanticism, a form of spilt religion, he reminds us of 'the solving emptiness/That lies just under all we do', in Larkin's unillusioned phrase. Not only is 'mother' in lower case but the faith that the speaker has in her is compromised by the strategic ambiguity of the word 'alone' in the line 'We place our faith in you alone'. Here the notion that the earth is all we have is subtly undermined by an alternative reading that hints that we may not even have that, that we are, ultimately, alone. This, you could say, is the 'astringency' that modernity imposes on any poet worth his 'salt'.

If in the metonym of the 'drop of the ocean' we can see a further attempt to accommodate extremes of scale, then something similar may be said for the image of the earth as a 'veined marble' at the beginning of the fifth stanza. The image expands and contracts at the same time as we attempt to hold together notions of the 'big wide world' and a child's toy. It also humanises the globe into a bio-sphere as rivers and coastlines are metamorphosed into veins. In case we might view Mahon's ecological aesthetic as a late development we might recall that he had already explored similar territory in 'An Unborn Child', an early poem in which the foetus is imagined 'Listening to the warm red water/Racing in the rivers of my mother's body'. This conception of a female topography is, as we have seen, fundamental to 'The Globe in Carolina'. We may even wonder whether there is a happy accident in the fact that the globe which the poet spins is in 'Carolina', a place name that also evokes a girl's name. There is indeed an

increasingly gendered inflection as male and female
participate in a metaphysical *hieros gamos,* or sacred
marriage:

> Veined marble, if we only knew,
> In practice as in theory, true
> Redemption lies not in the thrust
> Of action only, but the trust
> We place in our peripheral
> Night garden in the glory hole
> Of space, a home from home, and what
> Devotion we can bring to it.

It is instructive to compare these lines with W.H. Auden's
poem 'A Walk After Dark' and to speculate whether
Auden's nocturnal imagining may have influenced 'The
Globe in Carolina', albeit negatively. Auden's poem uses a
basic trimeter rhythm as opposed to Mahon's tetrameters,
and this gives a much lighter, almost frivolous feel to the
verse. The tone is chatty, confidential, relaxed:

> A cloudless night like this
> Can set the spirit soaring:
> After a tiring day
> The clockwork spectacle is
> Impressive in a slightly boring
> Eighteenth-century way.

The reader swings into step with the poet as he breezily
cuts the universe down to a more manageable size, referring
to 'those points in the sky' as 'the creatures of middle-age'

and comparing night itself to an Old People's Home, a conceit that the poet finds 'cosier' than anything more metaphysical. The poem goes on to explore the poet's commitment to political justice and to wonder, while 'the stars burn on overhead', what 'judgement waits/My person, all my friends/And these United States.' Clearly, we are not comparing like with like, but equally clearly Mahon's is the more grown-up poem. Auden is not really interested in the night sky except as a theatrical backdrop to his own reflections and he quickly loses sight of it in favour of some rather generalised musings on such standard Auden themes as time, truth and oppression.

By contrast Mahon is intensely interested in our place in the physical universe, conceiving of the earth as essentially organic –a 'peripheral/Night garden' – and space itself as an eroticised 'glory hole'. All this is in stark contrast to Auden's mechanistic image of space as a 'clockwork spectacle'. Moreover, while Auden gestures towards some unidentified shame and the prospect of retribution for wrongs done, Mahon unpicks with clarity and conviction the sorrow that informs his poem, identifying its source in the global technologies of war and waste. This becomes more apparent in the four stanzas that were excised from the original poem, where Mahon catalogues the environmental crimes perpetrated on the body of nature, culminating in the ominous image – redolent of Yeats's 'rough beast come round at last' – of 'the new thing that must come/Out of the scrunched Budweiser can/To make us sadder, wiser men.' The allusion at the end here to 'The Rime of the Ancient Mariner' is entirely relevant, Coleridge's poem being, as Hugh Haughton reminds us, 'about environmental violence, alienation and homecoming.'

The last two stanzas of the poem represent a subtle shift of perspective as the political gives way to the personal. Indeed, the reader initially experiences some confusion as to whom the 'You' at the start of the sixth stanza is addressed, whether it's a continuation of the prayer to the 'great mother' or an invocation of some other female presence. In fact, it soon becomes clear that the poet is invoking his estranged wife, Doreen, now living in Ireland. This adds a further poignancy to the poem as he imagines her not only on the other side of the model globe but on the slowly turning globe itself:

> You lie, an ocean to the east,
> Your limbs composed, your mind at rest,
> Asleep in a sunrise which will be
> Your midday when it reaches me;
> And what misgivings I might have
> About the final value of
> Our humanism pale before
> The mere fact of your being there.

The lines seems to offer a brief respite from the loneliness of the poet in his transatlantic exile as he links himself with his wife through the tender conceit of shared sunlight. However, the conceit simultaneously draws attention to the shared distance between them and the poem begins its gentle drift into the melancholy of the final stanza. Here we return to Carolina but to the real, existing Carolina and not the virtual one located on the globe. Reality, in other words, trumps any cartographical representation of it. It also brings the isolation of the poet into sharper focus as – unlike the creator figure hinted at in the first stanza – he contemplates his 'unfinished' creation : the 'desolate page', of the poem he is writing and which we are now reading. The soundtrack to his labours is neither Dvorak's 'New World' Symphony nor the birdsong suggested by Audubon but the mournful sound of a freight train heading for home:

> Five miles away a southbound freight
> Sings its euphoria to the state
> And passes on; unfinished work
> Awaits me in the scented dark.
> The halved globe, slowly turning, hugs
> Its silence, while the lightning bugs
> Are quiet beneath the open window,
> Listening to that lonesome whistle blow.

6

The Hudson Letter (1995)

FROM CAROLINA TO NEW YORK CITY, with a brief stop-off at a Dublin asylum and an artists' colony in Saratoga Springs, Mahon's trajectory in the thirteen years that span *The Hunt by Night* (1982) and *The Hudson Letter* (1995) describes an increasingly urgent quest for 'home'. By the time Mahon had become, officially, a 'resident alien' in New York he had lost his wife and two children through divorce, his base in Ireland and, it would seem, his poetic voice. 1991 saw the widely acclaimed publication of *Selected Poems*, but only one new poem from the fallow decade of the 1980s found its way into the collection. This poem was 'Dawn at St Patrick's', a wry, chastened account of a Christmas spent in Jonathan Swift's asylum for 'fools and mad'. The poem offers a particularly bleak *reductio* as the poet, 'with a paper whistle and a mince pie,/My bits and pieces making a home from home', attempts to salvage something from the wreckage of alcohol addiction. The phrase 'home from home' had been given a cosmological spin in 'The Globe in Carolina'; its reappearance here drags the poet away from metaphysical speculation back to the desperate immediacy of his own predicament. Nevertheless, a carefully measured poem came out of the experience and 'Dawn at St Patrick's' can be seen in retrospect as an important catalyst for the energised poetry he would write in America. A preview of what that poetry might look like may be found in 'The Yaddo Letter' (1990) where Mahon, exploiting again the resources of the verse epistle, introduces a looser, more colloquial idiom as appropriate to a letter to his estranged children. If the result is at times somewhat arch in its faux-naïf familiarity, it marks a significant shift away from the formal elegance of his more sculptured poems and paves the way for the rougher rhythms and more intractable structures of *The Hudson Letter*. (For reasons of space I shall not attempt to dicuss all the poems in *The Hudson Letter* – nor in the next volume *The Yellow Book* – but will focus on those that strike me as indispensable to any full understanding of Mahon's work).

The Hudson Letter – renamed 'New York Time' in *New Collected Poems* – is a sequence of eighteen poems cast in the form of an extended, polyphonic letter to his friend Patricia King. Based on his experience of living in New York it continues that excavation of the site marked 'home' which is clearly the dominant trope in Mahon's work. Yet if this preoccupation with home, homelessness and homecoming amounts almost to an *idée fixe*, it is one that is notable for its mobility and range. The poet's 'rented 'studio apartment' ... five blocks from the river' becomes the centre from which the poet travels out to those on the circumference of the American dream. The poet's location hints suggestively at the apartment forced on him by his separation from his family, while the word 'blocks' plays on notions of obstructed creativity. His temporary accommodation is compared to the country house of his dedicatee and in his imagination he contrasts the bright snow around her property with the less than glittering snow through which he walks on this winter morning. The setting is precisely evoked and gives us a powerful portrait of the artist as a not-so-young hobo, his self-identification with the homeless confirmed in the reference to Chaplin, the archetypal tramp:

> I often visualise in the neon slush
> that great heart-breaking moment in *The Gold Rush*
> where Chaplin, left alone on New Year's Eve,
> listens to life's feast from his little shack
> and the strains of 'Auld Lang Syne' across the snow.
> O show me how to recover my lost nerve!

The poet's failure to speak, to write, is emphasised only more by the continual noise of the radiators in his flat which 'knock, whistle and sing'. The word 'sing' prepares us for the introduction of the bird motif that runs throughout *The Hudson Letter*.

I toss and turn and listen, when I wake,
to the first bird and the first garbage truck.

The awkward chiming of 'wake' and 'truck' is part of the
acoustic dissonance which New York embodies, while the
juxtaposition of bird and waste carries, perhaps, echoes of
Eliot's 'Preludes' where a similarly disconsolate *aubade* is keyed
to the song of 'the sparrows in the gutter'. This collocation of
birdsong and the detritus of the city is explored more fully
further on in the sequence. For now, the poet welcomes the
music of 'Respighi's temperate nightingale' on the radio as a
reminder of the 'resilience of our lyric appetite' in the face of
such discords as the morning news. Then, picking up on the
earlier reference to 'the first bird', the poem concludes by
prioritising – 'but first the nightingale' – the claims of the
imagination, ending in true epic fashion with an invocation:
'Sing, Muse.' It is Mahon's answer to his own question at the
beginning of the poem: 'and what of the kick-start that should
be here?'

If 'kick-start' acts as a metaphor for a stuttering creativity,
it is literalised in the next poem, 'Out There', as it joins the
other cacophonous sounds that seep into the flat where Mahon
is working. We hear the 'stream of picturesque abuse' sent up
by 'some psycho' underneath his window, the 'hollering' of a
dog in the flat below, the noise above him of furniture being
moved, a 'whoop of police sirens, car alarms'. Even a 'love
scene on the sidewalk' is like something out of *West Side Story*,
while the racket made by an unseen 'hand' as it 'shook up the

empties in the recycling bin' is momentarily transformed into a poor man's *Rhapsody in Blue* by the 'Gershwin nonchalance' of the movement. A link is made here between music and refuse, with the implication that music, art, poetry, etc. are all various forms of recycled material. Mahon, we might say, puts the litter back into literature. Less facetiously we might recall Yeats's meditation on a similar theme in 'The Circus Animals' Desertion' where he locates the source of his art – 'those masterful images' – in 'A mound of refuse or the sweepings of a street,/Old kettles, old bottles, and a broken can,/Old iron, old bones, old rags, that raving slut/Who keeps the till.'

Mahon's more humane cultural materialism replaces the 'raving slut' with a cast of psychos, lunatics, paranoids, mad dogs, car thieves and a homeless alcoholic 'shivering for a drop of gin', all of whom are sketched with an understated compassion. If Mahon preserves a certain self-protective distance from those who are, in the poem's double-edged title, 'out there', the scene from his 4th-floor flat clearly exacts 'more interest' than the 'casual pity' of some of his earlier poems. Winter in New York forces him to consider the plight of those on the other side of the fence that separates the housed and the unhoused, the propertied professionals and those who 'gaze with satire or indifference/from cardboard boxes on a construction site'. The gap between rich and poor is the gap between cardboard and whatever concrete construction is about to overshadow them. The two worlds are worlds apart, yet within touching distance of each other, as we see – or rather hear – in the 'kick-start' of a motorbike at dawn. The noise stimulates a romantic fantasy about 'some heroine' – an ironic variant on the earlier 'some psycho' – who 'draws on her gloves for the Yamaha dream trip/to Provincetown, Key West or Sunset Strip'. The journey is described mock-heroically as an 'epic expedition' and the satirical tone helps to underwrite the poet's solidarity with the satirists who watch her from their flimsy shelters. Like the garbage men in Lawrence Ferlinghetti's poem 'Two Scavengers in a Truck, Two Beautiful People in a Mercedes' who gaze down 'as from a great distance/at the cool couple' in the car next to them 'as if they were watching some odourless TV ad', the outcasts of Mahon's poem survey a world of wealth and glamour in which they have no stake. The poem ends with an ambiguous *envoi* as Mahon watches those who, like his 'heroine', have the resources to escape from the city:

> To each his haste; to each his dreamt occasion.
> Nor snow, nor rain, nor sleet, nor gloom of night
> stays these swift couriers from their appointed flight.

The baroque rhetoric of these lines (with their ironic allusion to the motto of the New York City Post Office) sits uneasily with the poem's photo-realism, creating a tonal instability that reflects the shifting, feverish nature of a city that never sleeps. Exhaustion threatens to overwhelm the poet at his dawn vigil. He watches the 'Tired vents exhale; cloudy windows condense', sees 'vague vapours pearl fire hydrant

and chain-link fence' in a condensed linking that rhymes the
insubstantial with the solid.

This suggestion of fog, miasma, is continued into the next
poem, 'Global Village', where Mahon, walking through the
city at dawn and looking out beyond the 'abandoned piers/
where the great liners docked in former years', hears 'a foghorn
echo[ing] in deserted sheds'. Abandoned piers, deserted sheds
– places where a thought might grow. In this instance it is a
profoundly political thought: what is the reality behind those
images of global displacement – 'Ethiopian drought,/famine,
whole nations, races, evicted even yet,/rape victim and blind
beggar at the gate' – which 'will be screened tonight/on CNN
and *The McNeil-Lehrer News Hour*'? The foggy distortions
created by a media that blurs the distinction between news
and entertainment are neatly conveyed in the cinematic word
'screened', which not only conflates ideas of showing and
concealment but also, together with the word 'gate', reminds
us of the social and economic apartheid at the heart of the
global village. The use of the singular noun in 'rape victim
and blind beggar' also draws attention to the universality of
sexual violence and the perennial archetype of the outcast.
The mournful sound of the foghorn speaks more powerfully
of homelessness, poverty and loss than the image
manipulations of CNN. It also prompts Mahon to develop a
line of argument we saw in 'A Garage in Co Cork' as he
questions the basic 'look' of the city, peering past its post-
modern tenements to the 19th-century warehouses that made

New York the capital city of the world. The reference to the brooding figure of Hart Crane and a brief glimpse of 'a late flame flickering on Brodsky St' brings together two poets whose status as outsiders reminds Mahon of his own position as 'an amateur immigrant ... an undesirable resident alien on this shore'. His response to his new surroundings is ambivalent: he feels out of place, 'not being a yuppie in a pinstripe suit/but an Irish bohemian', and his alienation is caught in a snapshot of himself as 'a face in the crowd in this offshore boutique'. However, the city is not so easily dismissed; at the end it even seems to be in some sort of dialogue with the poet as the admonitory graffiti on a wall – 'LOVE ONE ANOTHER, RESIST INSIPID RHYME' – redirects Mahon back to his task, to his role as a lightning conductor for poetry. The poem concludes with a portrait of himself 'exposed in thunderstorms, as once before' yet still 'hoping to draw some voltage one more time'.

New York Harbour, pollution, waste, obsolescence, birds: the fourth poem in the sequence – 'Waterfront' – constellates some of the dominant themes of the first three. We are given the names of the great liners of the previous poem – '*Nieuw Amsterdam, Caronia, Île de France*' – whose 'fierce screws' once churned the waters as they docked. Now, however, the harbour has reverted to something less romantic, more entropic, the estuary 'adrift with trash and refuse barges', contaminated by 'infection and industrial waste'. This sea-change from the sexually charged 'fierce screws' to a more 'chaste' world where 'ice inches seaward in a formal dance' and the convalescent poet 'toddle[s]' into the cold water, parallels Mahon's recognition – taking his cue from 'old Heraclitus' – that one never steps into the same river twice. Change and decay in all around he sees, a sentiment with which this recovering, former hymn-singing Protestant would no doubt concur. Indeed, Americana is briefly interrupted by the Ulster voices of his boyhood as

> I recall my ten-year-old delight
> at the launch of a P&O liner in Belfast,
> all howling 'O God, Our Help in Ages Past',
> tugs hooting, block and tackle thundering into the tide.

The memory had been triggered by a sudden noise, the cracking of ice 'far off like a thunderclap/somewhere along Bohemia's desert coast'. One could read this as emblematic of Mahon's rehabilitation as a poet, the gradual thawing of ice in the 'warm snap' acting as a metaphor of recovery from addiction, of snapping out of a sub-zero inertia. What had once been static is now reanimated; the immobility evoked by the comparison of the winter scene to 'a lithograph/from *The Ancient Mariner*, from *Scott's Last Voyage*/or *The Narrative of Arthur Gordon Poe*' now gives way to present participle verbs: 'howling', 'hooting', 'thundering'. It is that moment in Coleridge's poem when, with the arrival of the albatross, 'The ice did split with a thunder-fit;/The helmsman steered us through'. Although no redemptive albatross appears in Mahon's poem – there's not even a 'Jersey blackbird' to 'serenade/this rapt scribe gazing from the Big Apple side' – nevertheless the mood at the end is delicately balanced between a millennial anxiety over what 'hot genes of the future' may be seething in the 'thaw-water of an oil drum' and the simple pleasure to be had from a winter sun that 'shines on the dump'. There's even another cryptic message on the wall to keep his spirits up: 'SUBVERT THE DOMINANT PARADIGM. GABRIEL 141'. The angel of New York has struck again.

Birds of one kind or another begin to make their presence felt more centrally in the next two poems in the sequence and we shall look at these poems together. In 'To Mrs Moore at Innishannon' Mahon adopts the voice and persona of a 19th-century domestic servant, Bridget Moore, who, having emigrated to the New World, writes a letter to her mother back in Co Cork. It is a vivid recreation of the diaspora experience of many Irish men and women who, like Bridget, found themselves on a boat bound for America. Her journey into exile is accompanied by a 'big gull' which 'sat at the masthead all the way', another variant on the theme of migration. The bird's journey, linking the two worlds, ends at Ellis Island with its disappearance into 'the mass'd rigging by the Hudson quays'. The word 'mass'd' not only suggests the anonymous crowd into which girls like Bridget would soon be absorbed but also makes a more nuanced point about Liberty's famous appeal to 'give me your huddled masses, yearning to be free'. The statue, symbol of New York, offers to compensate for the loss of home by standing in as a kind of surrogate mother, ready to shelter her many million children. Yet, as the quotation in the epigraph makes clear, the sculptor of the statue, Bartholdi, 'reacted with horror at the prospect of immigrants landing near his masterpiece', a reminder that the divisions in New York society which Mahon has identified begin at the threshold of the city.

The solitary 'big gull' that acts as a tutelary spirit in 'To Mrs Moore at Innishannon' multiplies into the Bronx seabirds that give the next poem its title. The birds are themselves former migrants, an exotic flock comprising 'Inca tern and Andean gull' whose escape from 'their storm-wrecked cage in the Bronx Zoo' invites the reader to consider what other kinds of jail-birds might wish to escape the 'system'. That 'system' is encoded in the electronic shorthand that introduces the poem as Mahon replicates the digitalised newspeak of a Times Square billboard, its unpunctuated headlines running into each other as the news accumulates like so much uncollected rubbish:

INSIDER TRADING REPORTS ARE LINKED TO PRICE OF BONDS NO SOLUTION AT HAND WHILE NUCLEAR WASTE PILES UP NEW YORK TOUGHING IT OUT TO GET THROUGH THE COLD QUESTION REALITY DEATH IS BACK NIGHT OWL GABRIEL 141 AT&T BOEING CHRYSLER DUPONT DIGITAL DOW JONES EXXON GENERAL MOTORS IBM NYNEX SEARS PARANOIA MCCANN ERICKSON AMERICA AFTER DARK ESCAPED BRONX SEABIRDS SPOTTED IN CENTRAL PARK ...

The language conveys the capitalisation of culture not only in its litany of commercial institutions but also in its upper case orthography. There is something almost apocalyptic in the way the rolling news keeps on rolling as criminality on the stock exchange merges with ecological disaster. Yet although the listing of financial markets and the proliferation of acronyms might suggest an entirely depersonalised corporate world, the text represents in disguised hexameter form that 'lyric appetite' whose resilience Mahon had extolled in the first poem. The 'radio serendipity' that had allowed the nightingale to be heard above the throng of other stations is paralleled here in the apparently random inclusion of another message from the alternative world of Gabriel 141. This time, as if to establish solidarity with the escaped seabirds, the angel of New York appears as a night owl and his message is typically dark and subversive: 'QUESTION REALITY DEATH IS BACK'. The death in question is a Darwinian one as New Yorkers and birds engage in an evolutionary struggle for survival.

The seabirds make the headlines through a technology that links them to the mania of the markets, yet their introduction into the body of the poem is through rhyme, ellipsis and a return to lower case sanity. The birds are described as 'a transmigration of souls', their migrant status a spiritual as well as a geographical one. Released by poetry from a solid block of digitalised prose, they sit in avian judgement on a world peered at through

mutant cloud cover and air thick with snow-dust,
toxic aerosol dazzle and invasive car exhaust,
or perch forlorn on gargoyle and asbestos roof,
fine-featured, ruffled, attentive, almost too high to hear
the plaintive, desolate cab horns on Madison and Fifth

The mixing of registers and acoustic effects here is characteristic of *The Hudson Letter* as a whole: the consonantal chaos of 'toxic', 'dazzle' and 'car exhaust' is counterpointed by the soft alliterations of 'forlorn', 'roof', 'fine-featured', 'ruffled' and 'Fifth'. Words like 'mutant' (with its SF connotations) 'aerosol' and 'asbestos' sit uncomfortably on the same poetic ledge as 'forlorn' 'plaintive' and 'desolate'. Ancient and modern vocabularies confront each other to produce a tone poem of considerable verbal complexity, one in which the 'almost too high' lyricism of the birds blends with the horns and motors below. It is tempting to read into this a covert defence of the 'high sentence' of Mahon's own metaphysically-inflected verse. Certainly his repeated use of nightingales as emblems of the 'lyric appetite' would imply a fundamental resistance to the grunge of contemporary culture. As he puts it in the central line of the poem, referring to the Bronx seabirds:

> like Daisy's Cunard nightingale, they belong in another life.

That sense of 'another life' puts them in the company of those who, like Daisy in *The Great Gatsby* and Ruth in Keats's 'Ode to a Nightingale' find themselves 'sick for

home', stranded among 'the alien corn' of New York.
Mahon's borrowing from Keats's poem extends to the
appropriation of words like 'forlorn' and 'plaintive', as if
he would situate his poem in the high Romantic tradition
of lament for a lost home. The homelessness of the birds is
poignantly evoked:

> They are intrigued, baffled and finally bored stiff
> by the wised-up millions lunching far below
> but vulnerable too as, askance, they stare
> at the alien corn of Radio City, Broadway and Times Square
> and up again at the clouds: where on earth can they go?

The question asks to be taken literally: there is nowhere 'on
earth' where these fugitives can safely belong since they are
'vulnerable' both to the toxic emissions of aerosols and car
exhausts and also to the waste products of 20th-century
consumerism: '"They won't touch garbage"'. The contrast
between the city workers at their lunch and the birds facing a
slow starvation – 'so where and what will they eat?' – leads
Mahon to make a direct appeal to the reader to get in touch
with the Manhattan Avian Rehab Centre, the word 'Rehab'
perhaps glancing at Mahon's own struggle to survive in New
York. He even gives us a telephone number and contact names
should we see 'one of these nervous birds'. It would be
interesting to know whether the number actually exists and if
Clare or Jill are indeed waiting to take our calls. The line
between fact and fiction, reportage and literature is blurred

here in a way that briefly reduces the poem to the level of agitprop or a Sunday morning radio appeal. However, the poem ends by returning us to the desperate plight of 'these rare species' in their competition with 'urban gulls, crows and other toughs of the air', the juxtaposition of 'toughs' and 'air' ensuring that the opposition between the Bronx and the birds remains unresolved.

The theme of migration is developed further in 'St Mark's Place' as Mahon follows in the footsteps of another New York émigré, W.H. Auden, a poet whose shambling appearance, alternative domestic arrangements and commitment to art are emblematic of that resistance to political and cultural hegemony which we have already observed. The portrait painted here is affectionate, yet the description of Auden as a 'slop-slippered bear' suggests something simultaneously endearing and endangered. Auden's eccentricities are set against the backdrop of the Cold War while the 'dirty window' through which the poet looks out onto Greenwich Village suggests the ideological murk of post-war American policy. Auden's years of exile transformed the poet from the former darling of the left to something less easy to define or, in some quarters, forgive. Mahon's sympathetic sketch of a fellow poet-in-exile highlights this shift from the political to the personal, suggesting that Auden's contrariness, heightened perhaps by his homosexuality, may be seen as a way of destabilising the prevailing moral consensus. Even Auden's Levi jeans – the ultimate American symbol – are described as 'dubious', a word that sums up the poet's sceptical stance towards a nation enamoured by visions of apocalypse:

> A disgrace
> to the neighbourhood, insistent on your privacy,
> what would you make now of the cosmic *pax*
> *Americana*, our world of internet and fax,
> an ever more complex military-industrial complex,
> situational ethics, exonerative 12-step programs,
> health fascism, critical theory and 'smart' bombs'?

The question is answered in a vision of an alternative society based on love and justice, on a recognition and acceptance of the otherness of others. The poet blends in with the underground commuters in a way that suggests an identification with those hidden from history:

> I see you ride at rush hour with your rich pity
> and self-contempt an uptown train packed to the doors
> with 'aristocratic Negro faces', not like ours,
> or reciting 'The Unknown Citizen' at the 'Y'.

The reference here to Auden's famous indictment of modern conformism is of a piece with Mahon's own embattled non-conformist sensibility. 'The Unknown Citizen' ends with a ringing defence of the individual in the face of an increasingly homogenised and sanitised society:

> Was he free? Was he happy? The question is absurd:
> Had anything been wrong, we should certainly have heard.

Instead of the unknown citizen's silence Mahon asserts, once again, the 'resilience of our lyric appetite' as he strains to catch the 'pure voice of elation/raised in the nightwood of known symbol and allusion'. Significantly, Auden is depicted as a presiding spirit in an 'unmarried' city 'so far from mothers'. In an earlier version of the poem Mahon had written 'so far from Mother', a more Audenesque locution, but one that invites a narrower, Freudian interpretation of the poet's sexuality. Freud is certainly invoked in the later reference to Auden prescribing 'a cure/for our civilisation and its discontents' but the lower case 'mothers' has the merit of broadening the perspective to include not only the orphans that haunt the singles bars of the city but Mahon's own separation from the mother of his two children. The poem ends with an appeal not so much to *eros* with all its attendant conflicts as to

> *agapè*, baroque opera, common sense
> and the abstract energy that brought us here,
> sustaining us now as we face a more boring future.

Exactly how baroque opera is going to sustain the urban poor is not made clear: 'check your privilege' one might say. Mahon's capacity for empathy, however, is not in doubt and in 'Alien Nation' we see him revisiting the plight of the dispossessed which he had earlier explored in 'Out There'. Indeed, the phrase 'out there' is casually slipped into the poem's evocation of life on or beyond the margins as the poet's own experience of 'alienation' – the word gestured to in the poem's ambiguous title – gives him an insider's insight into the deracinated world of the homeless:

> Clutching our bits and pieces, arrogant in dereliction,
> we are all out there, filling the parks and streets
> with our harsh demand: 'Sleep faster, we need the sheets!'

The sardonic humour here only intensifies the darkness that envelops the inhabitants of this world within a world, exiles who are barely recognised except as spectral figures on the fringes of the imagination. In a memorable description, the poet almost stumbles on them by chance:

> ... We come upon them in the restless dark
> in the moon-shadow of the World Trade Centre
> with Liberty's torch glimmering over the water

The chiaroscuro effect creates a brooding, film-noir atmosphere which heightens our sense of a city of extremes. The shifting, shiftless underworld of the homeless is briefly and ironically lit up not only by the glare of Liberty's torch but also by the neon tickertape of Times Square with its coded messages of consumption and decadence:

> RX GOTHAM DRUG GAY CRUISES SONY LIQUORS
> MARLBORO ADULT VIDEO XXX BELSHAZZAR DEATH
> IS BACK IGLESIA ADVENTISTA DEL 7MO. DIA ...

Mahon has, of course, used this framing technique before

in 'The Bronx Seabirds', but here the product placement and cultural allusions are, if anything, more pointed. New York merges into Batman's Gotham City, comic-book site of an elemental struggle between the forces of light and dark, while moral sleaze and the commodification of desire are vividly juxtaposed. Batman in turn morphs into Gabriel, dark angel of the city, whose minatory message – DEATH IS BACK – may be seen as a latter-day rewriting of the original writing on the wall. The apocalyptic note is continued with the reference to the Church of the Seventh Day Adventists, whose anticipation of the end-time ushers in the *Blade Runner* dystopia of an alien and ailing nation.

The language of the poem crackles with a kind of flickering energy borne out of anger and desperation. The high-minded, straight-laced tone of officialdom – as represented in the epigraph, a quotation from a leaflet on homelessness – is in stark contrast to the poem's mordant playing on words, titles and place names. The denizens of New York's *demi-monde* are 'glued to a re-run of *The Exterminator/*on a portable TV in a corner of Battery Park', the pun on 'glued' a reminder of the substance abuse that offers temporary consolation, while the choice of film and the reference to 'Battery Park' hint at abuse of a more violent kind. A sense of terminus, of coming to the end of the road, is concealed in *The Exterminator,* and also later in a reference to 'the Port Authority Bus Terminal'. There is, in addition, a subliminal distribution of 'x' and 'z' sounds throughout the poem which adds to our sense of the

brutalised, numbed experience of living on the streets. The
'XXX' of the tickertape is simultaneously a film certification,
a pornographic kiss and a sign of exclusion, while the 'x' at
the end of 'Bron*x*' and 'deto*x*' suggests a point beyond which
there is no return. Likewise, the 'z' sound in 'BELSHAZZAR',
evoking a hedonistic world of conspicuous consumption, is
deployed to more gritty effect in the picture of 'the de*s*ert of
cinderblock and ra*z*or wire' behind the Rit*z* Hotel and in
Mahon's self-consciously demotic identification with 'BAAAD
nigga*z* 'n' crack hoes on the rocks'. Mahon allows himself this
sense of a shared homelessness by placing it, typically, in a
wider context:

> Blown here like particles from an exploding sun,
> we are all far from home, be our home still
> a Chicago slum, a house under the Cave Hill
> or a trailer parked in a field above Cushendun.

Even conventional sites of displacement – the slum, the cave,
the trailer – are viewed, alternatively, as types of home relative
to the cosmic displacement of life itself. The poet's own
estrangements eventually take him away from his 'brothers'
in exile and back to the 'high loft' of the solitary imagination.
His transition from hobo to boho is enacted against the
backdrop of a makeshift nightclub where the dispossessed of
the city move 'under trippy light/smoke red and yellow where
the doctor spins/high octane decks among the boogie bins'.
This sulphurous, infernal world then dims as the poet feels

the first hint of a corresponding 'ocean breeze, flower-scented, soft and warm'. The profusion of sibilants in the line betrays a characteristic shift of attention away from the wasteland – human and otherwise – of history to a symbolic realm of aesthetic contemplation. Just as the speaker in 'The Last of the Fire Kings' longed to be like 'the man/Who drops at night/ From a moving train', so the poet in 'Alien Nation' also wants to be on the move, to escape the dissonance – the 'boogie bins' – of modernity by taking a yellow cab 'up Hudson St in a thunderstorm'. The fact that the cab driver is Haitian and 'mordant as Baudelaire' establishes a revealing synchronicity between the experience of exile and a notion of the poet as inherently, inescapably *maudit*. The thunderstorm, we might say, is a symbolic dramatization of a moment of crisis – we recall a similar charged moment at the end of 'Global Village' – as the poet exchanges the solidarity of the brazier for the lightning energies of art.

Such energies are given a specifically gendered inflection in the poem that follows: 'Sappho in "Judith's Room"'. Mahon's increasing engagement with feminism is channelled through an impersonation of the ancient Greek lyric poet Sappho whose cult of 'non-violent girls' provides an antidote to the patriarchal assumptions of 'Homeric bronze'. The poem wittily imagines Sappho reincarnated as a contemporary New Yorker, her fabled presence embodied both in her person and in her books on the shelves of 'Judith's Room', a feminist bookshop named after Shakespeare's putative sister in Virginia Woolf's

A Room of One's Own. The poem takes as its touchstone the same nightingale-inspired lyric voice that Mahon had evoked in the very first poem of the sequence and which had returned in later Keatsian or Ovidian contexts. Here it is as the harbinger of spring, in the recovery of that 'erotics of art' referred to in the epigraph's quotation from Susan Sontag, that the nightingale proves her resilience:

> The reed-voiced nightingale has been my guide,
> soft-spoken announcer of spring, whose song I set
> against a cult of contention I decried –
> except, of course, for 'the fight to be affectionate'.

That fight is a figurative one and a clear repudiation of the masculine heroics of epic poetry. In an appeal to Aphrodite, Sappho justifies her cult by asking 'what did I teach but the love of women?' The syntax – how do we read that 'of'? – delicately positions such love somewhere between a heterosexual and lesbian attraction, a freedom that allows her, as she says towards the end of the poem, to 'cling still to an old favouritism/or fall for a younger man from time to time'. For this former inhabitant of Lesbos, sex in the city takes the form both of an intellectual experience – reading to 'a thoughtful crowd' in the company of the great feminist icons of the sixties and seventies – and of a more immediate need for intimacy, eroticism, the pleasures of the body:

Girls, all, be with me now and keep me warm –
didn't I *say* we'd live again in another form?

Sappho's reincarnation is the latest example of recycling, her 'immortal work' a miracle of recovery as the fragments of papyrus on which her poems were written are 'exhumed from the Egyptian sands'. The revival of her cult in the 'other form' of twentieth-century feminism is perhaps a herald of a cultural spring, a much-needed renewal of the 'lyric appetite' which Mahon, like Sappho, finds in the 'reed-voiced nightingale'. The word 'reed' carries suggestions of both poetic and material metamorphosis as parchment and musical pipes combine to create a distinctive voice.

The last two poems in the sequence bear testimony to Mahon's continued preoccupation with survival and resilience, a concern mediated in 'St Bridget's Day' through an extended address to Jack Yeats – writer, painter and father to his more celebrated son, William – and then in 'Rain' through a return to the theme of homelessness that has been the central leitmotif for *The Hudson Letter* as a whole. In 'St Bridget's Day' we overhear one half of an imagined dialogue with the 'pilgrim father' whose letters to his son the poet has been reading. The poem touches on the now-established theme of the artist in exile, torn by competing versions of 'home'. For Mahon the need to escape from 'the turbulence of this modern Rome' and catch an aeroplane that will take him back to Ireland is complicated by the perspective offered by the 747's descending flight as it touches down to 'the cabin crew's soft '*failte*'/and

the strains of "My Lagan Love"'. The Gaelic word *failte*, or
'welcome' and the traditional song that accompanies the poet's
imagined arrival – it should be recalled that the Lagan river
runs through Belfast – create a powerful set of associations
for a poet who presents himself, in a phrase that combines
religion and addiction, as 'a recovering Ulster Protestant from
Co Down'. His projected homecoming, however, fails to bring
him the sense of belonging he was hoping for. Instead, he
cuts a rather forlorn figure, an ex-poet and rapidly ageing
man in 'an old mac/with the young audibly sneering behind
my back'. In Philip Larkin's poem 'Afternoons' a similar sense
of a life unlived among the swings and sandpits of a children's
park leads to an elegiac meditation on time and the losses it
brings. We learn that the wind is 'ruining the courting places'
of the young mothers whose beauty has 'thickened' as their
children 'push them' – a telling reversal – 'to the side of their
own lives'. Mahon likewise – 'deafened by seagulls and the
playground cries/of children' – records his own displacement
in lines that are delicately balanced:

> Now, listening to the *rus-in-urbe*, spring-in-winter noise
> of late-night diners while the temperatures rise
> and the terrible wind-chill factor abates, I realize
> the daffodils must be out in ditch and glen
> and windows soon flung wide to the spring rain.

The return of warmer weather prompts the speaker to
compare the relatively mild conditions in Ireland with the

more extreme climate in New York, and leads him to reflect on Yeats's obduracy in 'negotiating the icefields of 8th Avenue/ to die on West 29th of the "Asian flu"'. The tone is admiring, a salute across the pond from one homeless artist to another. More significantly, the conventions of the verse-letter allow Mahon to engage his addressee in an informal conversation about art's relationship to the world, a central preoccupation in Mahon's poetry.

St Bridget's Day, 1 February, marks the start of the Celtic spring (or Imbolc, the poem's original title) and it is instructive to note the many and varied roles that the saint plays in Celtic mythology. Among other things she is the patron of children, fugitives, Ireland, nuns, poets, scholars and travellers. Her appeal to the fugitive artist and Irish émigré, J.B. Yeats, is clear in his compassionate response to the homeless mother and child from Donnybrook he met one day on New York's riverside. Her exiled status places her with the Biblical figure of Ruth, that archetype of the displaced and the dispossessed, whom Keats in his 'Ode to a Nightingale' situates 'among the alien corn'. The phrase is carried over into Mahon's poem and the nightingale association is continued with a quotation from one of Yeats's letters:

> 'The nightingale sings with its breast against a thorn,
> It's out of pain that personality is born.'

This insight into human suffering – 'your epiphany' – allows Yeats to soften his son's rigid distinction between the man that suffers and the mind which creates. For Yeats *père*, art is a commitment to a humane awareness of others, to 'the human face ... and the priority of the real.' However, this awareness is part of the wider remit of art as, essentially, a form of magic or gnosis. Mahon quotes Yeats as saying: 'Art is dreamland' and it is this dual perspective of art as something both rooted and transcendent that gives the artist his self-divided identity. Mahon goes beyond the blue plaque simplicity of 'Yeats, Artist and Writer' to get to the heart of his own contradictions:

> may we add
> that you were at home here and in human nature
> but also, in your own words, lived and died
> like all of us, then as now, 'an exile and a stranger'?

It is precisely because he is 'like all of us' that J.B. Yeats becomes, for Mahon, an exemplary figure, a type of the artist who manages to be simultaneously inside and outside society.

The amphibious nature of the artist's calling is explored in some detail in 'Rain', the final poem in the sequence, where the poet compares his youthful desire to be off and away – 'Once upon a time it was let me out and let me go' – with what Hugh Haughton calls a 'dream of belonging' that sees him clamouring at the end to be let in from the big freeze of a New York winter:

> When does the thaw begin?
> We have been too long in the cold. – Take us in; take us in!

The poem is bookended by notions of 'out' and 'in', with the fairytale beginning –'Once upon a time' – casting doubt over the reality of his earlier vagrant self. However, if Byzantium is no country for old men – and the shade of J.B. Yeats's son haunts the margins of this poem – then New York is even less hospitable to those 'drifters, loners ... [who] come knocking late', desperate to return to 'the enchanted garden in the lost domain'. The latter phrase borrows from the title to the English version of Alain-Fournier's *Le Grand Meaulnes* – that exemplary statement of romantic longing – and there is clearly a personal context to Mahon's plea for readmission to 'the house, the stove in the kitchen, the warm bed,/the hearth, *vrai lieu*, ranged crockery overhead'. However, there is also a self-conscious bracketing of the domestic dream that prevents the poem from becoming merely an exercise in nostalgia. A sense of the interiority of art – 'the vigilant lamplight glimpsed through teeming rain' – is matched by an attentive turning outwards to the world beyond 'felicitous space'. It is significant that the poet in his Manhattan apartment has 'one window slightly open to let in the night air', allowing him to 'peer down through the fire escape' at a city based on 'superfluous light', a kind of film set city complete with its 'all-night populations' of the homeless. In a few deft brushstrokes Mahon delineates a world where the glare of 'searchlights and dead stars' exposes the brutalist architecture of New York and the equally brutalist economic system that supports it, a system that finds its most symbolic expression in the aptly named 'Trump Tower'. This concrete hymn to private wealth dominates the skyline, yet it is only the most visible manifestation of a spiritual sickness that seems to penetrate every strata of society, from the United Nations to

> the halls of finance, the subway walls of the brain,
> the good, the bad, the ugly and the insane,
> the docks and Governor's Island

The chiming of 'halls' and 'walls', the image of the brain as a subway, the cinematic reference to a tale of gunslingers competing for gold, the addition of insanity to the list of ills, and the twinning of commerce and government all serve to establish a complex critique of American values. Who is 'in' and who is 'out' in a society founded on property is a central concern in the poem. Those on the outside, who have 'no homes to go to but their eternal one', are confronted by 'the chained door and the locked gate', the word 'gate' half-rhyming cruelly with 'unfortunate' in the next line, while towards the end of the poem Mahon returns to the theme when he says: 'I think of the homeless, no rm. at the inn'. The Christian allusion universalises the situation, the rejected Christ-child becoming the prototype of outsiders everywhere, while the reduced, abbreviated form of the word 'room' points to the way language itself encodes its own system of exclusion. Just as there was little 'elbow room' for the 'lost people of Treblinka and Pompeii' in 'A Disused Shed in Co Wexford', so there is little room – even in the word 'room' – for the 'lost and the disappointed' of New York.

Faced, then, by a society in which power and privilege are enshrined, the poem seeks to locate an alternative source of meaning in those materials that make up our physical and cultural lives. Moving from the scene outside his window to the artefacts in his apartment Mahon observes an interior world of 'lamp, chair, desk, oil-heater and bookcases/brisk with a bristling, mute facticity'. A disconnected, atomised humanity is contrasted with 'the greater community/of wood and minerals throughout the city' as objects, including art objects, are recycled and thereby given a kind of permanence:

> When the present occupant is no longer here
> and durables prove transient, as they do,
> all will survive somehow; the pictures too,
> prints, posters, reproductions ...

The poem goes on to identify the pictures on the wall of the apartment, ranging from the Italian Renaissance to American pop art, and including photographs and collages. What appears at first to be a somewhat arbitrary collection turns out to have a direct bearing on Mahon's preoccupation with art as a continual process of recycling. All art objects, the poem implies, are reproductions, not just the ones that are sold as such. Botticelli's *Birth of Venus* itself enacts a rebirth, a renaissance, her Greek name Aphrodite recycled into its Latin form. Similarly, the Roy Lichtenstein print ('B ... but, Brad ... ')

may be seen as an attempt to deconstruct comic book conventions in order to reconstruct them into something else, a procedure that informs all pastiche and parody. As we have noted before, Mahon's own extensive use of quotation and allusion is part and parcel of the same *modus operandi*, and extends to some quite drastic revisions of his own work. What saves Mahon's poetry from being a cut-and-paste assembling of parts is the abiding concern with the human subject in her fleeting relation to time, her sense of her own temporality. We see this in the final picture referred to in the poem as Mahon concludes his guided tour of the apartment:

> and (look) my favourite, over there on the right,
> picked up at a yard-sale in Connecticut,
> Kroyer's *Women on the Beach*, a hazy shore,
> their footprints in the sand to the waterline,
> the human presence since we live here too –

The print on the wall reproduces another kind of print: the human footprint that disappears even as it is memorialised in paint. Significantly, the picture had been salvaged from a scrap-yard, a striking example of the universal will to survive which Mahon tentatively celebrates as he watches for 'springtime and the lengthening days'.

The poem ends, however, on a sombre note and a widening of perspective as the loss of friends and contemporaries prompts Mahon to consider our final destination, our ultimate home. Yet even as he prepares to lie at night 'empty of mind, the heart at peace', folded into the '*dark mother, cave of wonders*', into the 'interior of the rose', he cannot forget –as he reminds his dedicatee, Patricia King – that 'the voyage is never done'. The poem enacts a dynamic that takes him inwards in the company of his 'guardian angel, best friend', but also out to 'the gaseous planets where they spin,/the starlit towers of Ninevah and Babylon'. The claims of art and the spiritual life, heard in 'the secret voice of nightingale and dolphin', are counterpointed by a vison of 'fish crowding the Verrazano Bridge', a phrasing that recalls Yeats's 'mackerel-crowded' sea. The conflict between monument and flux, centre and circumference, can perhaps never be fully resolved in the mind; nature herself appears undecided as Mahon sees 'even in the icy heart of February,/crocus and primrose'. We have reached the end of *The Hudson Letter*, yet that last image takes us back to the place where, in a sense, it all started, in Carrowdore churchyard, where a young poet observed 'the ironical, loving crush of roses against snow'.

7

The Yellow Book (1998)

WHEN *THE HUDSON LETTER* WAS PUBLISHED in 1995 it met with a mixed response. Some reviewers pointed to a certain slackening in the verse, a discursiveness that compared unfavourably with the tautness of Mahon's previous poems. However, its heterogeneous, bric-a-brac nature is what makes it such a remarkable volume and, in my opinion, one of the great long poems of the twentieth century. Its unevenness is arguably a strength, not a weakness, allowing for a much more varied treatment of its material. Critics also noted the exposed, confessional quality in the poems, frequently invoking Robert Lowell as a presiding spirit, and praising or damning accordingly. Mahon himself, however, had already moved on, geographically and artistically, by the time *The Hudson Letter* had been posted; his next volume, *The Yellow Book*, was to prove a less intimate, more satirical collection, its sights fixed firmly on the turn of the century *zeitgeist*, its publication date two years short of the Millennium.

The Yellow Book marked the poet's return to a Dublin enjoying a rare moment of economic and cultural prosperity – the so-called 'Celtic Tiger' phenomenon. Mahon's *fin-de-siècle* sequence of twenty poems draws attention in its title to its nineteenth-century namesake – the house magazine for an aestheticism that gave to the 1890s its distinctive look, sound and smell. That earlier decade had seen a decisive shift in values as poets and artists, playwrights and set designers, *flâneurs* and assorted dandies followed the example of Wilde, Whistler and Beardsley, among others, in rejecting the conventional wisdom that Art imitates Life. On the contrary, what Art reveals to us – as Wilde puts it in his 1899 essay *The Decay of Lying* – is 'Nature's lack of design, her curious crudities, her extraordinary monotony, her absolutely unfinished condition ... When I look at a landscape I cannot help seeing all its defects'. To make good those defects writers and painters of the period self-consciously privileged artifice over nature, style over substance, sophistication over sincerity, town over country. The result was not only the hot-house interior of des Esseintes' heavily perfumed room in Huysmans' *À rebours* – the novel thought to be the original 'Yellow Book' referred to in Wilde's *The Picture of Dorian Gray* – but also the rarified atmosphere of French Symbolist poetry and, in turn, Modernism. From

Decadence to Mallarmé to *The Waste Land* is a line of development that has, in hindsight, a certain logic.

Mahon's own version of *The Yellow Book* may be seen as an attempt to update the conversation started by Wilde and those other writers (Dowson, Johnson, etc) who were later dubbed by Yeats 'the tragic generation'. In the 1890s that conversation centred on a fundamental resistance to what was perceived as an entrenched philistinism at the heart of English society. Looking primarily to France for their models, the poets sought in the celebration of the senses – Dowson's 'madder music and stronger wine' – an alternative to the arid rationalisms of bourgeois society. (It is no coincidence that the decade saw a revival of interest in Keats). The period also witnessed a conflict between two distinct notions of art: the aristocratic (or at least hieratic) and the demotic. When Yeats, at the end of the century, attended a performance of Alfred Jarry's *Ubu Roi* he was shocked to see the king carrying a toilet brush in place of a sceptre. He later recorded his feelings in a valedictory review of his own aesthetic models:

> After Stephane Mallarmé, after Paul Verlaine, after Gustave Moreau, after Puvis de Chavannes, after our own verse, after all our subtle colour and nervous rhythm, after the faint mixed tints of Conder, what more is possible? After us the Savage God.

A hundred years later we see Mahon in characteristic oppositional mode establishing a similar kind of dialectic between two versions of decadence: on the one hand, that of the Baudelarian *poète maudit*, staring out of his attic window at a dark, symbolic sky; on the other an aggressive modernity that threatens to ruin 'the work of years'. The first poem in the sequence, 'Night Thoughts', finds the poet in pensive mood as he lies in his Dublin flat 'smoking between three and four/before the first bird and the first tour bus.' The juxtaposition of bird and bus establishes the two basic values in the poem's equation: just as at the beginning of *The Hudson Letter* the poet had woken to hear 'the first bird and the first garbage truck' so at the beginning of *The Yellow Book* Mahon occupies a liminal space that briefly accommodates both inner and outer, art and life. As so often in Mahon's work, the *aubade* is the occasion for a certain kind of childlike wonder at a dawn world revealed in all its rain-washed innocence. He remembers similar mornings as a child 'wide-eyed in an attic room behind the shore/at some generic, gull-pierced seaside town'. The poem goes on to retrieve a miscellany of memories that link the adult poet to his younger self in a way that recalls Proust's pursuit of lost time:

> Each white shoe you can remember, each stair-rod,
> each streaming window on the Antrim Road,
> a seaside golf links on a summer night,
> 'pale sand-dunes stretching away in the moonlight'.

The reverie is broken by the appearance of a horse-drawn cab in the Georgian square below his window, a reminder of the heritage industry that threatens to turn the past into an ersatz version of itself. In this poem of re-habitation Mahon wanders back to the end of the previous century, imagining his attic room as a place where 'maids slept in the days of Wilde and Yeats'. The construction work going on outside interrupts such sleep and sets up a conflict between different kinds of light: the harsh crane-light of machines and the dawn light that 'whitens a locked park, lilac and hawthorn/dripping in wintry peace'. The *hortus conclusus* behind the railings is described as 'absorbed ... in its own existence', a state of self-communion – of *l'art pour l'art* – that could equally apply to much of the poetry of the 1890s. A fear of contamination, of pollution, lies at the heart of aestheticism; Mahon acknowledges a similar fear when he lists in the same line 'crocus, daffodil, air brake and diesel-chug', the ugliness of the last word inscribed in the word itself. Mahon's satirical gifts are evident in his portrait of modern-day tourists as 'aliens, space invaders ... goofy in baseball caps and nylon leisurewear'. Mahon's response to the ugliness of contemporary life is to reaffirm the 'self-delighting' principles of a poetry born from 'Sententious solitude, ancient memory, night/and silence'. In this mood of detachment it is possible to forget the coaches thronging the square, the exhaust fumes, the shouts under his window, the cranes and the brick-dust, and, instead, 'switch on the fire, kick off your shoes/and read the Symbolists as the season dies'. The poem ends with a translated fragment from Laforgue's 'L'hiver qui vient', an act of literary homage to one of the many late 19th-century writers who haunt the pages of *The Yellow Book.*

Included in this company is the anti-hero of Villiers de l'Isle-Adam's 'Axel' who lives and dies in a remote castle in the depths of the Black Forest – though 'lives' is hardly the right word for someone who says of life: 'Our servants will do that for us'. This latter exponent of the hermeticism that characterises much of the literature of the 1890s provides the reference point and title for Mahon's second poem in the sequence: 'Axel's Castle'. (The title is also a nod to Edmund Wilson's notable study of the period.) All the details are in place to recreate, albeit ironically, a late 20th-century version of 19th-century Symbolism. There is the dusk setting – Eliot's 'violet hour' – as the pre-condition for a certain kind of crepuscular meditation, a twilight of the mind in which Athena's owl, symbol of wisdom, can fly; there is the poet sitting at his desk in his attic study, looking down at the garden in Fitzwilliam Square, imagining a world beyond the iron railings, a world unknown to commuters as they hurry home to the suburbs; there is a sense of waiting patiently for the moment when the dried-up fountain, the silent pavilion and the dead leaves in the park – emblems, perhaps, of the poet's own inactivity – give way to a state of mind in which the external world dims in the unnatural glare of lamplight; there is the privilege and privileging of writing and 'the pleasures of the text' – some 'langorous prose' – that puts him at odds with modern technology; there is also a reminder of the personal, psychological cost of living so far removed from the world, both spatially and figuratively:

> The psychiatrist locks up and puts out the light
> on desk and couch in his consulting rooms.
> It's cold up here in the city of litter and drums
> while fires glow in the hearths of suburban homes.

One reason why Mahon is drawn to the world of the *fin de siècle* is, I would suggest, a sense of kinship with those writers and artists of the period whose lives were ruinous, brief, or both, whose self-destructive decadence was aided and abetted by the 'artificial paradises' that led to addictions of one kind or another. As Holbrook Jackson puts it in his wide-ranging study *The Eighteen Nineties*:

> Most of [the writers] died young, several were scarcely more than youths; some died of diseases which might have been checked or prevented in more careful lives; some were condemned to death at an early age by miserable maladies, and some were so burdened by the malady of the soul's unrest that they voluntarily crossed the borderland of life.

Mahon's own struggle with alcoholism has been well documented. At the time of writing *The Yellow Book* he had officially dried out yet the addictive personality is only ever dormant and may take any number of forms. The northern Irish Protestant in Mahon might reject the theatrical props associated with the Decadent movement –

the peacocks and porphyries, the poppies and lilies – yet something, or someone, is equally if not more alluring:

> A foxy lady slips into her shoes
> and leaves me words of wisdom

The allusion to 'Mother Mary' in the Beatles' song 'Let it Be' conflates secular and sacred to create a composite figure of Muse and divine inspiration. As if to demonstrate the superiority of that inspiration over reality, the triumph of armchair vision over 'cheap flight', the poem embarks on its own virtual tour of the globe. Mahon alludes to an episode in Huysmans' novel *À rebours* where des Esseintes reconstructs a ship's cabin in his own kitchen in order to simulate the experience of travel, without actually having to go anywhere. This is followed by a litany of places Mahon regrets not having visited, though he consoles himself with the thought that 'imagination can get you there in a tick/ and you're not plagued by the package crowd'. Here is the central conflict – not just in this poem, but throughout Mahon's work – between art and life, imagination and modernity, a conflict embodied in the demotion of the 'holy city' to a mere tourist destination. Although Mahon doesn't identify this sacred site, it is clear that Yeats's 'holy city of Byzantium' is the model, not least in Mahon's longing for 'a Byzantine privacy in mews and lane.' The reference to the 'high window ... showing one studious light,/somebody sitting late at a desk like me' manages to bring together Mahon, Milton's 'Il Penseroso', Yeats and Larkin in silent conversation. The light itself is 'studious', a transferred epithet that suggests the absorption of the poet in his own work. The poem ends elegiacally as Mahon registers a shift in aesthetic values as Dublin's past is all but effaced by the demands of a consumer society:

> mostly now the famous Georgian doors
> will house a junk-film outfit or an advertising agency.

The words 'junk' and 'outfit' are strategically placed, conveying not only disdain but a profound resistance to the new cultural order. Although the flute music of the fountain in Fitzwilliam Square is silent, traces of the past remain, notably in the Yeatsian image of 'the beeches with their shades of Coole demesne'. However, this echo of an earlier time, of an 'old decency', is drowned out by technology, as 'computer talks to computer, machine to answering machine'. In this dystopian scenario, Mahon's description of himself as a 'diehard' carries a painful resonance.

Throughout *The Yellow Book* the same minatory note is sounded: that a technologically driven society, where machines talk to machines, is fundamentally inhospitable to art. Mahon's stylish take on the 1890s – a decade that witnessed the valorisation of style above all – is itself a way of affirming that even in the 1990s style is still the man. One man in particular who had the courage to flaunt a revolutionary aesthetic in the face of the public was, of course, Oscar Wilde. In a review of Richard Ellmann's biography of Wilde Mahon seeks to rescue the Irish playwright from his popular caricature as a 'highbrow Noel Coward' and to enlist him in the culture wars of the new *fin de siècle:*

> Like Rimbaud, [Wilde] insisted that art should be absolutely modern; yet it's only now that the nature of his example is becoming clear. His involvement with the 'pre-Raff', his feminism and socialism, his use of style as a weapon, have, as several critics have pointed out, a proleptic higher punkdom about them ... which will make him an apt *maître-a-penser* for our own '90s. It's a measure of Wilde's complexity that we should have had to wait a hundred years to understand, to be *allowed* to understand, exactly what he was about.

Wilde's 'higher punkdom' is the focus of the next poem from *The Yellow Book* that we shall consider: 'Rue des Beaux Arts'. The title establishes the setting as the street in Paris where Wilde died – impoverished, ill and haunted by the sexual scandal that led to Reading Gaol. The poem is in the second person, a direct address from one 'old trendy' to another that allows for an intimacy of tone, a familiarity even, that fits the hushed ambience of a room where 'you doze most of the day with curtains drawn'. Mahon's identification with Wilde – another 'yellow-journalism survivor' – extends to a close examination of his drinking habits: his social downfall is encapsulated in the exchange of 'the silvery tinkle of champagne' for 'muddy clouds of absinthe and vermouth'. The heady days of the original *Yellow Book* are recollected in the description of 'the new art' with its 'whiplash line/derived from pre-Raff ivy and twining vine', the contorted rhyme at the end and the distribution of long 'i' sounds throughout setting up a decadent music that is momentarily undercut by the short, sharp shock of 'whiplash'. It is as if, latent within this world of sensory and aesthetic pleasures, a punitive morality is waiting to exact retribution. Which it was.

Morality, moreover, is now joined by Nature herself in a predictable return of the repressed. Affronted by Wilde's disparagement of her, she seems intent on restoring the *status quo* in the relationship between Art and Life, with Art very much the inferior partner. An increasing sense of a man at the mercy of a woman scorned pervades the poem:

> it's mid-July and nature has crept back
> to the rue des Beaux Arts and the rue du Bac,
> the humid side streets of the Latin Quarter
> with its rank plants and warm municipal water,
> its fiery pavements scorching feet and soul

The conventional contrast between town and country is here magnified into a conflict between Paris – home of the *beaux arts* – and something approaching a South American jungle. No wonder Wilde's curtains are drawn when even the light of the afternoon is described as 'hot-house'.

The agonies of Wilde's 'yellow fever' are only eased when dusk falls over the city, allowing him to 'take/[his] walk by

the twilit river'. Like a true *flâneur* he wanders through the
city, pausing to visit a church, browse in Galignani's
bookshop or even mix with the tourists. Wilde's
estrangement from his wife and children – a situation
Mahon himself was all too familiar with – is perhaps behind
his wistful observation of schoolchildren in the
Luxembourg Gardens, while the reference to 'infants piping
in the Coupole' is a direct borrowing from Eliot who in
turn borrowed the line from Verlaine, a poet whose
troubled personal life – desertion of family for a young
man, imprisonment, death in a Parisian garret – in many
ways mirrors that of Wilde. Indeed, Wilde himself
acknowledged the parallel, stating that 'the century will have
had two vagabonds, Paul Verlaine and me'.

Wilde's vagabondage, given the century he lived in, could
only end in defeat. A melancholy hangs over the poem as
Wilde faces his own ruination, a physical and spiritual death
evoked in the mournful 'aw' sound of the lines:

> The morgue
> yawns, as it yawned too for Verlaine, Laforgue,
> nor will you see your wife and sons again.

Yet this 'old windbag' (as Mahon calls him) has enjoyed
a remarkably successful after-life as a writer whose
transgressive sexuality and cultural iconoclasm answers to
contemporary needs. The repeated 'still' and the demotic
idiom in 'Still full of hot air,/still queer as fuck and putting
on the style' relocates Wilde to the 1990s and reverses the

original verdict of the court, the newspapers and public opinion:

> ' *The thing now is to forget him; let him go*
> *to that limbo of oblivion which is his due* –
> though the *Daily Chronicle* and the *St James Gazette*
> are gone, while you are talked of even yet.

The point is made, irrefutably, by the rhyming couplet. The rest of the poem presents Wilde in a half-ironic, half-religious stage-light. It is impossible to read the description of him as 'backlit by sunset' without recalling Wilde's withering denunciation of sunsets in *The Decay of Lying*:

> Nobody of any real culture ... ever talks nowadays about the beauty of a sunset. Sunsets are quite old-fashioned. They belong to a time when Turner was the last note in art. To admire them is a distinct sign of provincialism of temperament.

More acceptable to Wilde would be the way the sunset is transfigured by Mahon's art into something more interesting: 'grotesque tableaux' where 'unprecedented creatures' are 'printed there/in angelic purple-and-gold photography/and the stars shine like gaslight'. Stars like gaslight, the natural compared, unfavourably, to the artificial – once again Nature is given only a supporting role in the great comic drama of life. Except that by now the comedy has taken a distinctively dark turn as Mahon draws a parallel between Wilde and other suffering outcasts:

> Job with a skin rash and an infected ear,
> Oisín in the real world of enforced humility,
> you pine still for the right kind of solitude
> and the right kind of society;

Mahon gestures briefly in the last line to Wilde's eccentric brand of radical politics – as expounded in *The Soul of Man under Socialism* – before returning to the central dialectic in Wilde's thought:

> but it's too late
> to benefit from the astringency of the sea
> or come to terms with the nature you pooh-poohed;
> for you, if anyone, have played your part
> constraining nature in the name of art,
> surviving long enough for the birth-knell
> of a new century and a different world.

Mahon's poem ends with a beginning as Wilde's ghost – 'the party's life and soul' – entertains the dead in the afterlife. It is a fitting conclusion to a spectacular career that ended in apparent failure. However, as the last line reminds us, quoting another last line, the last words of Ellmann's biography of Wilde:

> *'The greatest men fail, or seem to have failed.'*

Wilde, as we know, put his talent into his work and his

genius into his life. In 'To Eugene Lambe in Heaven' Mahon provides a more recent example of a similar self-fashioning in the form of a Trinity friend from the 1960s whose cultivation of an extreme aestheticism in manners and dress earns Mahon's unqualified approval. If Mahon is, in the words of Tom Paulin, 'an intransigent aesthete who rejects life almost completely and considers only the flotsam and jetsam along its fringes', then Eugene Lambe was a similar refusenik, 'an exiled Stuart prince', one of nature's aristocrats among the 'savages/of the harsh north'. His status as a counter-cultural hero, a latter-day Wilde complete with velvet smoking jacket, sets him apart as a member of that exclusive club of 'perfect writers who never write,/a student of manners and conversation straight/from the pages of Castiglione or Baudelaire'. Like Wilde, however, Lambe's resistance to the normative world of middle-class aspirations ends in loneliness – 'your castle of indolence a monastic den' – and eventual death from a heart condition that is seen as symptomatic of a wider societal pathology. As the sixties gave way to the seventies and the seventies to Thatcherite economics, so the pursuit of wealth in an 'age of sado-monetarism' – a cruel play on words that conflates sexuality, power and money – replaces the kinder values embodied in Eugene Lambe, who at the end of the poem has been simultaneously materialised and transfigured into 'the stuff of myth'.

The ghost of Wilde continues to haunt *The Yellow Book* in the next poem we shall consider: 'Hangover Square'.

The title, a nod to Patrick Hamilton's study in inebriation, foreshadows the poem's concern with – and defence of – the twin palliatives of art and alcohol. The poem also takes up Wilde's fairy-tale figure of the Selfish Giant and places him, transformed into a snowman, in 'a far corner of the square' from where he stares back at the children who made him. The snowman is clearly a type of the isolated poet whose 'abstract mien and cold bituminous eye' marks him out as an outcast, one of those 'old boys' – a telling oxymoron – 'who 'ate the altar rails, pawned pride for drinks/or tumbled from high stools in the Rose & Crown'. Mahon's identification with both the snowman and those 'desperate characters' of the 1890s – Dowson, Johnson and, of course, Wilde himself – is a statement of allegiance to more than just a style. It is, he says, a way of 'proclaiming a different order of reality/from the bright children who gave rise to him'. Mahon presents himself not as among school children but as totally apart from them, a selfish giant 'made to freeze and rule/the garden as if self-generated there'. He has become an 'ex-child at the window watching them,/specs on his nose and winter in his eyes'. Yet if the price paid for a poetry perfected in sub-zero temperatures is an 'organism dark with booze and nicotine' then the price, it seems, is worth paying. In choosing perfection of the work Mahon has refused not only the 'heavenly mansion' but the humble home as well. The cost and rewards of such a refusal are spelled out in lines that link Mahon with his *fin-de-siècle* predecessors:

Owning like them 'an indolent, restless gift',
fitful, factitious and at best makeshift,
burning without warmth or illumination,
each verse co-terminous with its occasion,
each line the pretext for a precious cadence,
I keep alight the cold candle of decadence.

Cadence/decadence – the connection could not be
clearer. Mahon's mastery of 'the singing line', the musical
resourcefulness of his verse, is the result of a willingness to
trade ordinary happiness – the common dream – for
something more 'precious'. That word is poised, however,
among competing values: a cadence is 'precious' in that it
is of great price, like a precious stone; it is also costly,
perhaps in human terms; it can suggest something over-
refined or affected; it can even mean something of little
worth as in 'you can keep your precious poetry'. Mahon is
no doubt alert to all these nuances. Indeed, the poem ends
with a recognition that to oppose 'rhyme-sculpture' to the
'entangling vines of nature' is 'a futile project', given the
way modern technology threatens the very existence of the
book. The final lines give us a portrait of the artist as a
Luddite, bashing away at his old electric typewriter, each
letter printed one at a time, 'fuzz round the edges'. Of
course, 'the edges' is exactly where Mahon has chosen to
position himself for most of his writing life.

Such distancing provides Mahon with a perspective on
modernity that allows for an increasingly satirical take on
contemporary forms of decadence. One poem in particular

– 'At the Chelsea Arts Club' – has the dyspeptic tone of an updated *Dunciad* as Mahon makes an implicit contrast between the 'junk culture' of the 1990s and the more refined aestheticism of a hundred years earlier. Mahon is caught in something of a cleft stick: while he laments the loss of 'significant form' in the commercially driven art products of the late 20th century he also has to avoid sounding like a retired colonel, harrumphing about the young and their appalling music. The tension is there from the beginning of 'At the Chelsea Arts Club' where the first lines – 'Everything aspires to the condition of pop music,/the white noise of late-century consumerism' – gesture towards both Walter Pater and Oasis. The pale oils of Whistler's Thames are lost in the 'gleam' of a more brash and brazen century as Mahon reveals a morbidity, a death-wish even, under London's surface glitter: the chrome of cars on the embankments is 'exhausted'; traffic moves at 'funeral pace'; violence and sensationalism are encoded in 'body art, snuff sculpture, trash aesthetics,/the video nasties and shock computer graphics'. The Arts Club, once home to Wilde and Whistler, still accommodates 'the sniftery dandies at their studied poses,/the eyepatch woman and the monocle man' – Beardsley characters straight out of the original *Yellow Book* – yet it also now houses art installations like 'Tank Girl', a fetishised human mannequin with a taste for bondage. Mahon portrays her as 'the Muse in chains, a screw bolt in one ear,/the knickers worn over the biking gear ... ' The chained Muse is an appropriate icon for a culture that would restrict and debase the arts to the level of kitsch or pornography. Mahon's reaction to contemporary decadence is, fundamentally, reactionary:

> Maybe I'm turning into an old fart
> but I do prefer the traditional kinds of art,
> respect for materials, draughtsmanship and so on –

What Mahon also prefers is the chaste atmosphere of the Chelsea Arts Club 'in the afternoon when the bar is shut', when the smoking room – 'an empty Chekhov set' – yields to 'silence, buttery light,/euphoria and nostalgia'. The second half of the poem takes the form of a litany in praise of all things yellow, from crocuses to Manhattan taxis, bananas to pencils, as well as things which, if not actually yellow – in what sense is magic realism yellow? – have an aesthetic quality that makes them suitable for inclusion in Mahon's expanding Yellow Book.

Yellow is also the colour of nicotine-stained fingers and the next poem to consider, 'Smoke', is cast as a meditation on the one addiction remaining to Mahon after he had stopped drinking. It also serves as a fitting conclusion to this group of self-consciously 'Decadent' poems. Again, the *mise-en-scène* is an early evening, rain-washed Dublin seen from the perspective of Mahon's top-floor flat in Fitzwilliam Square. We have the customary distancing of the poet from the world beyond his window in order to 'concentrate on pipe dreams and smoke clouds'. This is the 'proper dark' which Yeats had enjoined Irish poets to climb into, and Mahon takes the advice quite literally, mounting the stairs to the top of his own Thoor Ballylee. His chosen stimulant may now be cigarettes, not alcohol, but a fastidious aestheticism informs his ritualistic preparations:

> 'Turkish on the left, Virginia on the right',
> my cigarette a lighthouse in the night.

As we have seen, the lighthouse has featured as an emblem of artistic isolation in other poems but here the symbol is miniaturised to create a strong sense of the encroaching darkness lapping at the poet's desk. The darkness takes various forms, from the poet's own Coleridgean dejection to environmental disasters and cultural decline as toxic smoke from a 'contagious bonfire of the vanities' drifts across a corporate landscape dominated by 'Klein and Nike, Banana Republic, Gap'. However, the 'clouds of glory' produced by the poet's cigarette are part of an alternative history and defense of smoking as Mahon – 'blue in the face behind my veils of smoke' – tries to 'recapture pool dreams or evoke/aesthetic rapture, images of felicity'. Those images have a distinctly middle eastern or oriental inflection; they include references to Camel cigarettes, Xenophon in Persia, the quest for eastern trading routes, the mist on Monet's 'nebulous nenuphars' (a type of lotus flower), a Tiepolo ceiling in that most oriental of European cities, Venice, and finally a glimpse into Rick's, the smoke-filled night-club in the film

Casablanca. This paean to an eastern culture of smoking stands in sharp opposition to the prevailing puritanism of the west, even if, ironically, it was America that gave tobacco to Europe in the first place. In lines that remind us of Mallarmé's dictum that he liked to keep 'a little cigarette smoke between [himself] and the world', Mahon defends the habit of smoking as a source of

> inspiration, aspiration, hope,
> lateral thinking, 'pure speculative ether',
> an apolitical sphere above the weather.

Now, however, smoking has becoming so politicised that 'even on death row,/even in the electric chair tobacco is taboo', the aural closeness of 'tobacco' and 'taboo' underlining the shift in attitudes. The prohibition stems from a suspicion of anything that has no use, that is its own justification, or which 'suggests alternatives to the world we know/and is to that extent consoling'. The poem ends with three different *exempla* from the long history of smoking: Lady Bracknell's statement in *The Importance of Being Earnest* that 'a man should have an occupation of some kind'; Walter Raleigh's attempt to find the weight of smoke – 'perhaps even of the soul' – by weighing cigars against cigar ashes; and the Russian formalist Bakhtin, a victim of Stalin's early purges, recycling his own manuscripts into cigarette paper. Such recycling is yet another instance of the intimate relationship between art, pleasure, language and silence 'as we exhale/clouds of unknowing with our last gasp.' The art of smoking, like the art of the Japanese tea ceremony, can bring the true devotee to the edge of wisdom.

Before we leave *The Yellow Book* it is important to stress that the collection as a whole is not as narrowly focused on *fin-de-siècle* poetics, Decadence and other pre-millennial concerns as the poems we have looked at might suggest. The scope is wider than that and the volume as a whole more varied. There are pen portraits of figures as diverse as Elizabeth Bowen, Schopenhauer and J.G. Farrell, further satirical swipes at contemporary 'barbarism', a wonderful poem about a dead bittern 'destroyed by thirst', and a moving if restrained elegy for Mahon's mother whose collection of bric-a-brac is seen as a counterpart to her son's predilection for unconsidered trifles. Yet despite the variegated tones of the collection, the volume is held together by a basic attitude of intransigence, a kind of bloody-minded resistance to anything that smacks of a cultural consensus. Resistance, however, if it is to be more than a gesture, needs its own aesthetic. For Mahon that aesthetic takes the form of an increasingly urgent dialectic of waste and recycling, a conviction that, to quote the title of the Blur song, modern life is rubbish.

'Christmas in Kinsale', the last poem in the sequence, has the feel of a postscript about it as if it too were part of a surplus economy of found objects, along with the rest of the rubbish the poet takes out on a Christmas morning in County Cork. The inventory of household waste includes

the wet and dry, the cardboard and the trash,
remains of rib and chop, warm cinders, ash,
bags, boxes, bulbs and batteries, bathroom waste,
paper and tinfoil, leaves, crumbs, scraps and bones –

In their accumulation of materials these lines become the verbal equivalent of a landfill site, a piling up of refuse that is at the same time an attempt to dispose of it, or at least bring some kind of order to it. This is achieved through a combination of balanced phrasing, antithesis, polysyndeton, alliteration, rhyme and metre – in other words the full repertoire of linguistic resources available to the poet. What appears a random miscellany of waste products is, when looked at more closely, an example of the sorting and sifting of rubbish that is the first stage in the recycling process. These fragments may not only be shored against the poet's ruin, but also against the ruinations of history, as the reference to 'vestiges of a distant past' suggest. That past includes Kinsale itself – site of a decisive English victory over the Irish at the turn of an earlier century – and, more remotely, the calendar changing events two millennia ago in Bethlehem which the poem commemorates. Stitched into the fabric of the poem are local details that remind us that the context for the poet's Christmas morning visit to the bins is, initially, a Christian one: bells ring out 'through dispersing mist/from the Church of Ireland and St John the Baptist'; smoke rises 'like incense' from a chimney; angels and scribes are half-glimpsed in the trees, and there is 'a continuous chorus of divine praise'.

As the poem progresses, however, the divine praise acquires a more secular inflection as Mahon's litany of waste extends to include the natural world. He imagines the 'clouds of flies/buzzing for joy around the rubbish bins' in the summer, the words 'joy' and 'rubbish' brought together in an unexpected relationship. Mahon, too, is surprised by joy at the sight of snails and peonies, of 'an iridescence in the sea breeze,/a bucket of water where the rainbow ends.' There is a growing awareness and acceptance of end-time now, a mood of apocalyptic peace, as nature becomes the site where 'the harsh will dies', far from the 'elsewhere' of 'tough cities,/the nuclear wind from Windscale, derelict zones'. Here, by contrast, Mahon records

> the triumph of carnivals, rinds and skins,
> mud-wrestling organisms in post-historical phase
> and the fuzzy vegetable glow of origins.

From post-historical back to pre-historical the wheel of the Great Year turns, a Yeatsian trope that Mahon recycles in the final image of the cock crowing 'from an oil drum/like a peacock on a rain-barrel in Byzantium'. This is Yeats's golden bird from 'Sailing to Byzantium' but with important differences. Mahon's bird is not an abstract, symbolic bird but a peacock, emblem of that vanity the preacher in 'Ecclesiastes' denounced. Nor is it 'set upon a golden bough to sing' but instead is perched alternately on oil drum and rain-barrel, images of toxicity and life respectively. Mahon's rewriting of Yeats is a genuine recycling of materials that allows for a more inclusive vision of perishability and a more representative audience. Instead of the hammered gold of art we have soap-bubbles that 'foam in a drainpipe and life begins'; instead of an audience of lords and ladies there is merely a middle-aged poet taking out his rubbish; instead of a bird singing 'Of what is past, or passing, or to come' we hear only the cock crowing 'good-morning'. The poem ends where Yeats said all responsibilities begin – in dreams. Mahon returns to a dream of 'a blue Cycladic dawn', a dawn of ancient Greek beginnings that reminds us of the cycles of history, the wheel of birth and death, a dawn that holds out an invitation to the dance as the poet hears 'again the white islands shouting, "Come on; come on!"'

8

Collected Poems (1999)

MAHON'S *COLLECTED POEMS* WAS PUBLISHED one month short of the Millennium, a date which the poems in *The Yellow Book* had approached with varying degrees of foreboding. Although a largely retrospective overview of forty years' work, several new poems appeared, including a number inspired by a recent visit to Italy – another destination to add to Mahon's impressive collection of places where a thought might grow. Among these Italian poems 'Roman Script' is the most compelling, combining a dizzying virtual tour of the Eternal City – home to 'the beautiful and damned', from the in-crowd in Harry's Bar to deranged emperors and debauched popes – with an insistent probing of the relationship between representation and reality. Mahon opposes the 'art historical sublime' of the Sistine Chapel – its frescos wittily transformed into a 'violent comic strip' – to the flash-photography of a lightning storm that reveals 'Cecilia's actual body, Endymion's actual grave', the latter being in fact the grave of Keats. The poem ends with a homage to the murdered film director and 'poet of poverty', Pasolini,' whose actual body on the beach at Ostia takes its place among 'the bright garbage on the incoming wave'. In another example of the textual recycling that Mahon's poetry enacts, the last line recast the poem's Italian epigraph – *Nei rifiuti del mondo nasce un nuovo mondo* – into English: 'in the refuse of the world a new world is born'. The poem comes full circle, returns to its own linguistic source in Pasolini's own poetry, an implicit acknowledgement that all art, all life, is a continuing process of (re)translation.

The need for rebirth, albeit on the 'peripheral rubbish dumps beyond the noise/of a circus' begins to occupy a central place in Mahon's work as it moves from the middle-period survival aesthetics of *The Hudson Letter* to a rejuvenated late phase, one that is clearly announced in 'A Swim in Co Wicklow'. It is this poem I wish to look at now before we consider 'St Patrick's Day', the last poem in the collection.

It might be fanciful to suggest that one of Mahon's former incarnations was a fish but it is a fancy worth exploring in view of the extraordinary number of references to water in his poetry. Mahon is so often to be found walking on the seashore – usually at dawn – or dreaming of the sea or gazing at it from a distance or listening to it crashing on rocks or crawling up the beach from it that it is clear that, more than any other element, water exerts a primal pull on his imagination. Not just the sea but rivers too, as we saw in the poem 'Waterfront' in *The Hudson Letter*. There the poet, one of the 'chaste convalescents' who 'come to rivers when we are young or old', had 'toddled' into the water in an attempt to cool his 'cabin fever'. He imagines that Heraclitus, philosopher of flux, famous for observing that we never step into the same river twice, is there at the scene too.

We see a similar need to immerse oneself in water in 'A Swim in Co Wicklow', whose epigraph from Montale – *The only reality is the perpetual flow of vital energy* – prepares us for the poem's own vital energy in producing the kind of 'mouth music' we tend to associate more with Heaney. This cleansing of the senses in the waters of language perhaps reaches back into memories of the poet's Church of Ireland childhood, with its baptisms and holy water. Philip Larkin, required to construct a new religion, imagined a liturgy that would use 'images of sousing,/A furious devout drench', and there is in Mahon's account of his swim in Co Wicklow a similar sacramental quality, a mysticism of the body that amounts to a rebirth. Having 'come back once more/to this dazzling shore' Mahon likens the experience to that of an embryo enjoying the 'warm, uterine rinse' of the womb, a conceit that Mahon had explored earlier in 'An Unborn Child'. This rinsing of the self allows the subject to experience itself as a 'you', a reminder that, in Rimbaud's formulation, 'Je est un autre':

A quick gasp as you slip
into the hissing wash,
star cluster, dulse and kelp,
slick algae, spittle, froth,
the intimate slash and dash,
hard-packed in the seething broth.

This is language at its most densely auditory, a
soundboard of onomatopoeia, alliteration, assonance,
consonantal and vowel clashes, slant and internal rhymes,
mixed registers. To read it aloud is to experience an almost
physical participation in the thing being described. It leaves
us breathless and a little afraid as the body records its own
mutation into the marine life that surrounds it. The violent
acoustics of this 'hard-packed' stanza then modulates in
the next into a softer music as the subject adapts to its new
watery environment. Language is eroticised in the 'sensual
writhe and snore/of maidenhair and frond', the word
'maidenhair' carrying associations of both virginity and
seduction. The poet feels 'the close tug of origin' as he
reprises his biological role as a 'rogue gene', origin and
gene half-rhyming together in the poem's evolutionary
progression.

This poem of beginnings also has a corresponding sense
of an ending. The white conch on the pebbled beach, eroded
by the 'suck and crunch' of the sea, is described as a 'sandy
skull as old/as the centuries', echoing Mahon's dream poem,
'Day Trip to Donegal' where the sea 'washed against my
head,/Performing its immeasurable erosions –/Spilling into

the skull'. Here, though, the dream is a 'waking one', with little of the nightmarish quality of the earlier poem. Instead there is a sense of elemental freedom, playfulness, a living in a 'today' where

> you swirl and spin
> in sea water as if,
> creatures of salt and slime
> and naked under the sun,
> life were a waking dream
> and this the only life.

In 'Ecclesiastes' the preacher had promised 'nothing under the sun' as part of a world-weary, life-denying religious ideology. Here the phrase 'naked under the sun' has a quite different complexion, allowing for a transformed sense of material well-being, a sense that nakedness is no longer a source of shame but of intense pleasure as the body is re-baptised into the flow of life.

However, just as we are getting used to a more 'chilled out' Mahon, someone who now enthusiastically embraces the modern injunction to 'go with the flow', so old habits of resistance and opposition reassert themselves in 'St Patrick's Day', the last poem in the 1999 *Collected Poems*. Part portrait of Swift, part verse letter to Patricia King, the poem moves between an 18th-century Trinity College, home to Ireland's most famous curmudgeon, to a contemporary St Patrick's Day celebration with all its attendant horrors. Mahon imagines the 'grim ghost' of Swift

pacing the long library, a figure whose bodily complaints –
'vertigo, sore ears and inner voices' – are matched by an
equally pained sense of atrophy in the public sphere, with
the Yahoos of *Gulliver's Travels* transported forward in
time to the Dublin stock markets, the whole country, in an
ironic glance at Prospero's more mellifluous isle, 'full of
intolerable noises'. At the start of the second stanza the
New Age pleasures of nude bathing invoked in 'A Swim in
Co Wicklow' are briskly cancelled out as the body becomes
a site of suffering:

> Go with the flow; no, going against the grain
> he sits in his rocking chair with a migraine

The caesura in the first line is strategically placed, while
the triple rhyme of 'go', 'flow' and 'no' and the
uncomfortable alliteration of the hard 'g' sound in 'going',
'against', 'grain' and 'migraine' – the last two words chiming
so exactly as to mimic the repeated thumping of a headache
– all enact a poetics of struggle and resistance. Too infirm
to ride out to 'bubbling stream and weir,/to the moist
weather and white belvedere', Swift's compound familiar
ghost, deprived of the healing sources of water, settles for
the more complex consolations of satire, denouncing the
'confederacy of dunces and mohocks' that passes for an
intelligentsia and venting his spleen ('scholars and saints
be d-mn'd') at the slave mentality that results in submission
to a 'hard/reign and our own miniature self-regard'. Rain
has hardened into 'reign', nature into history, and the

denizens of Lilliput/Ireland are revealed in all their smug, small-minded limitations.

The poem continues to splice older versions of Irish history with more recent narratives, mixing up the centuries to provide a palimpsest of myth and modernity. Leaving Swift and his complaints behind, Mahon finds plenty of opportunities to exercise his own splenetic gifts as he and his companion plunge into a city in the grip of national celebrations. Against a soundtrack of ghetto-blasters he laments the 'new festive orthodoxy and ironic icon' that allows the Celtic past, represented by Niamh and Oisín, to be projected onto a screen, 'their faces lit up like the Book of Kells'. The hybridisation of culture intensifies in the next stanza with a typical Mahon list of sights and sounds in which Bridget's daughters mingle promiscuously with 'wizards on stilts, witches on circus bikes,/jokers and jugglers'. This is no country for middle-aged men like Mahon, the poem implies, nor for those who look over their shoulders to the rain-soaked, priest-ridden Ireland of the past:

> We've no nostalgia for the patristic croziers,
> fridges and tumble-dryers of former years,
> rain-spattered cameras in O'Connell St,
> the sound mikes buffeted by wind and sleet –

The verse breaks off as if Mahon has to snap out of his own reveries, conscious of the woman by his side whose birthday it is. He glances at another kind of birthday too as he recalls how in New York – 'under a shower of hail' – they had watched 'post-Christian gays cavorting up Fifth Avenue'. The memory provokes thoughts of his own 'coming out' as a 'recovering Ulster Protestant from Co Down', his status as a 'rueful veteran from the gender wars' and this new relationship between 'a Sacred Heart girl and a Protestant rogue.' The stanza ends with the delicately balanced metaphor of 'chill sunshine warming us to the very bone,/our whole existence one erogenous zone'.

The final two stanzas confirm Mahon's credentials as a cultural critic in verse, a terminal ironist contemplating the anomaly of writing in a 'post-literate' world. Self-mockingly, he portrays poetry as a matter of 'structures and devices', of 'fancy flourishes and funny voices', a poor relation to the more glamorous products of the 'audio-visual realm'. Poetry is seen, wryly, as an anachronism, a symptom even, a temporary stage in the transition from 'the ancestral dream' to the 'vast corporate scheme/where our true wit is devalued once again'. We are back again with the Yahoos on their mobiles, 'triumphant in the market place'. If this sounds elitist it is because it is, but it is an elitism born of despair at a society that creates its own ghettos of privilege and power. Mahon's poetry has always hesitated between the high Romantic and the demotic, its registers shifting often alarmingly between the two. But this instability of language is part of a more fundamental instability in reality itself, however defined:

> The one reality is the perpetual flow,
> chaos of complex systems.

This insight is at the heart of Mahon's poetry and is one that he has pursued with remarkable energy and consistency: 'so back to the desktop and the drawing board'. It allows him to attend to the present moment even as it vanishes 'like snow/off a rope, frost off a ditch, ice in the sun'. He is the celebrant of all that does not remain, that stays for a moment and then departs. He has the humility to remove himself from the frame so that we can get a clearer glimpse of 'prismatic natural light, slow-moving cloud,/the waves far-thundering in a life of their own'. It is a humility that allows him, as he moves into the next stage of his creative life, to see, in 'a young woman hitching a lift on a country road' an image of all those, like himself, who have no homes but their eternal ones.

9

Harbour Lights (2005)

*H*ARBOUR LIGHTS IS ARGUABLY THE MOST satisfying book of Mahon's late-blossoming career, winning him the Poetry Now Award in 2006. Awards and prizes, however, have never been of paramount importance to Mahon; he has maintained a principled position on the edges of the literary world, an aspect of his general resistance to, and rejection of, an increasingly commodified culture. The words 'resistance' or 'resist' occur nine times in the opening poem 'Resistance Days', another chatty and intimate verse letter, this time to his friend, the photographer John Minihan. Writing from Paris in the 'post-Christmas lull', Mahon interweaves memories of his student days in the 'sexy city' with recent impressions of Morocco, where Mahon had gone to escape the horrors of 'corporate Christendom'. Morocco thus becomes another *vrai lieu*, an alternative to the 'murderous tedium/of business culture', a place where he can sing carols with 'a lost tribe of Nigerian *sans papiers,*/bright migrants from hot Sahara to cold EU/in the leafy English church Sam Beckett knew'. Mahon again identifies himself with a 'lost tribe' (a phrase he had used in 'Nostalgias' for the Ulster Protestants of his youth) while at the same time expressing an affinity with a fellow Irish writer-in-exile.

The idea of 'resistance' has, of course, a specific nuance in the context of French history; Mahon extends it to include a broad cultural opposition to the creeping corporatism represented by 'the damned logo everywhere you look', an allusion to the ubiquitous McDonald's sign. Mahon resolutely sets his face against anything that smacks of the *ersatz* and the inauthentic, valorising instead the 'real' in 'off-line France' or in Tangier with its 'peach-pink Arabian nights, the call to prayer/on Lavery's dunes and balconies, austere/as antelope or ibex, a light as rare.' Even the old typewriter on which he writes his verse travelogue and the 'snail mail that can take a week' to deliver it are part of his defence of a slower, more contemplative relationship to 'reality', however defined. To this end, he aligns himself with other *refuseniks,* dissenters who have rejected the cultural consensus, radical figures like William Burroughs and Allen Ginsberg, or Wyndham Lewis – 'a real barbarian ... in flight/from daily mail, tube station and wireless set' – or those in the existentialist tradition of Sartre and de Beauvoir. In Morocco he finds, quoting Patti Smith, 'the real earth of Rimbaud', while in Paris he celebrates 'real tomatoes, real *brioche*/and real stars like Adjani and Binoche'.

Throughout the poem Mahon establishes a conflict between two competing notions of reality based on two kinds of representation. Mahon has long been fascinated by the visual arts, finding in them analogues to his own practice as a poet. We saw this in 'Courtyards in Delft', and in many of the poems in *Harbour Lights* we see a similar engagement with the fundamental question of art's relationship to the real. In 'Resistance Days' Mahon distinguishes the 'shinier compositions' of commercial photography from 'the glow/and heartening realism' of the photographs of Robert Doisneau. In these Mahon discovers something more authentic, more humane:

> (industrial suburbs, the great aerial one
> of the Renault plant beside the Bois de Boulogne,
> pensioners, tramps, young lovers in a park,
> a kiss at rush hour or a dance in the dark)

Mahon, the most Heraclitean of modern poets, finds a justification for his own poetry of flux in the 'flash photography' of heat-lightning in a summer storm. In contrast to the glossy, airbrushed aesthetics of post-modernity, Mahon's verse has a raw, unpredictable energy as one verbal snapshot follows rapidly aupon another to create 'an art as fugitive as the life it snaps'. The word 'fugitive' is important here, combining ideas of ephemerality with notions of flight and homelessness.

Mahon thus becomes a student of the fleeting reality of 'weather, clouds and their formation', following Gerard Manley Hopkins, another keen watcher of the skies, who recorded his observations of clouds in his journals and in his great poem 'That Nature is a Heraclitean Fire and of the Comfort of the Resurrection'. Mahon's poem, stripped of theology, extols 'the real chaos of indifferent nature' and ends with a quiet affirmation of the private self that comes close to the quietism of Eliot's *Four Quartets*:

> Down silent paths, in secret hiding places,
> the locked out-house that no one notices,
> listening for footfalls by a quiet river
> the sun will find us when the worst is over

The vexed question of art and reality also informs the next poem in *Harbour Lights*, the Yeats-inspired 'Lapis Lazuli'. Mahon's poem not only borrows – or rather steals – its title from Yeats's poem of the same name, but is even dedicated to a poet who happens also to be called Harry Clifton. Thus, from the start, Mahon invites us to consider issues of authorship and ownership, the recycling of materials, an inquiry that centres on 'this azure block blown in from the universe' which acts as a paperweight on the poet's desk. Even something as dense as this 'piece/of planet rock' is 'still shimmering', alive in the same way that the 'swirling sea' and 'slowly moving cloud' are alive. It is, says Mahon, 'the real thing in its natural state,/the raw material from which art is born', an acknowledgement of the use to which painters throughout history have put the stone's exquisite blue pigment. There is a timelessness about the stone – 'it never dates' – that reminds us of the 'place out of time/a palace of porcelain' in 'The Last of the Fire Kings', the difference being that while porcelain is delicate and easily broken, the stone is 'coarse-grained and knobbly as a meteorite'. In this poem, at least, authenticity trumps art. The prospect of spending 'days of silence, watching as paint dries' leads to a privileging of slowness – 'slow fires', 'slow thought' – as a necessary pre-disposition for the cultivation of inwardness, here represented by the young woman who 'reads alone in a lighted train' in the last stanza. Her stillness offers hope for a world where 'planes that consume deserts of gasoline/darken the sun in another rapacious war', a clear reference to the invasion of Iraq in 2003. As a calm alternative to the 'hysterical women' of Yeats's poem, she is one of those 'loved women of our private myths', the embodiment of an eco-feminism that had become increasingly important to Mahon .

We see this in the next major poem in *Harbour Lights*, 'The Cloud Ceiling', another poem that owes much to Yeats. The latter's 'A Prayer for my Daughter' is clearly behind Mahon's poem but there are important differences. Instead of the lofty 'May she ... ' of Yeats's poem, 'The Cloud Ceiling' is written in the form of an intimate, second-person address to his baby daughter, Maisie. (Mahon was by now in a new relationship). Yeats's appeal to custom and ceremony as antidotes to 'the great gloom that is in my mind' is replaced by what Hugh Haughton calls Mahon's 'romantic biologism'. Yeats's anxiety for his daughter's future in a fractious Ireland is countered by Mahon's holistic faith in nature as essentially benign, a universal womb that nurtures all her children. The poem moves from the moment of conception through to the formation of the foetus and the emergence of a child 'given to light readings and rich inactivity,/alternative galaxies, atonal composition/and tentative revisions of quantum gravity'. This is a child wholly at home in her microcosmic world, whose cloud-decorated ceiling stands in for the sky itself: 'The indeterminate firmament is yours'.

The poem is suffused with images of clouds, water, sea, grazing sheep, 'a splash of stars' while the use of the word 'of' in phrases like 'daughters *of* ocean' , 'grave sisters *of* the rainbow, rose and iris' emphasises that sense of indwelling that had eluded Mahon in his earlier work. That the birth of Maisie has had a transformative effect on Mahon is clear in the final stanza where he describes his own (re)birth in the waters of life:

> I who, though soft-hearted, always admired
> granite and blackthorn and the verse hard-wired,
> tingle and flow like January thaw water
> in contemplation of this rosy daughter.

'The Cloud Ceiling' is a brave poem in that it risks being embarrassing. The language is sometimes deliberately childish and whimsical. But just as Joyce mimics the lisping speech of the child at the start of *A Portrait of the Artist as a Young Man*, so Mahon reaches back, through onomatopoeia, assonance and alliteration, to something primary in language itself:

> So drench the nappies; fluff, bubble and burp;
> I probably won't be here when you've grown up.

The last line – with its imperfect rhyme – is particularly effective in tempering the exuberance of the poem with a more sombre intimation of mortality. Mahon knows that 'happiness writes white' and treats his readers at the end to a satisfyingly 'grown-up' conclusion.

So far, then, the poems in *Harbour Lights* have addressed by now familiar themes: the natural world as a habitation and home, a commitment to the flux of life as the reality out of which art is made, the need to resist the consensus of modernity, the dismantling of patriarchal values in favour of a more feminised reading of the world. A further theme, that of waste, has been central throughout Mahon's career and returns in 'During the War', a rain-soaked view of London's Soho. We are given another glimpse of the rejuvenated Mahon as he forgoes the run-down lift in his block of flats, preferring to 'bounce on sneakers up a winding stair', a rather cheeky appropriation of the Yeatsian symbol. A stone's throw from Blake's birthplace, Wardour Street is portrayed not as part of some New Jerusalem but as a mess of roadworks and puddles:

This morning in Wardour St, a skip, a tip,
a broken pipe, some unfinished repair work.
A basin of mud and junk has choked it up,
reflecting the blown sky and a baroque
cloud cinema beyond earthly intercourse.

In contrast to Yeats's patrician disdain for the raw
materials of creativity – 'the foul rag-and-boneshop of the
heart'– Mahon has, as we have seen, a positive relish for all
things coarse, discarded or overlooked, a fascination with
the detritus of urban life:

This is nothing, this is the triumph of time,
waste products mixing in the history bin,
rain ringing with a harsh, deliberate chime
on scrap iron, plastic and depleted tin

Into the history bin also goes a film crew whose strip
lighting 'writes the dusk out everywhere', the ubiquitous
'porn and veg' of sleazy Soho and the surface rainwater
whose 'rippling skin' is 'mutating by the minute', a complex
image that fuses together ideas of change, natural
phenomena and human flesh. The poem ends with a
brilliant description of the hole in the road as 'a shivering
dump with one faint star in it', the reflected star both a
counter to the artificial light of the film set and a gleaming
sign of redemption at the heart of a throw-away culture.

Mahon's peripheral vision – his eye for the overlooked –
leads him to inhabit the hidden lives of those who occupy
the margins. He is arguably one of the finest practitioners

of the self-revealing dramatic monologue since Browning. 'Jean Rhys in Kettner's' is a good example of his empathetic imagination, a vividly realised portrait of the artist as a young woman, 'crouching here in the corner' of a Soho wine-bar with a gin and cigarette. Jean Rhys, author of *Wide Sargasso Sea*, a prequel to *Jane Eyre*, is deftly sketched to evoke her rackety, bohemian life in cold, draughty England, alongside warmer memories of a Caribbean childhood. Clearly, Mahon finds her an intriguing figure, someone who was, like him, 'in at least two minds' as to where she belonged. The image of her at the end of the poem as 'a torn bag in a thorn-field/snapping and scratching, fighting to keep sane' captures her lonely, uncomfortable existence and reminds us of the tree in 'Going Home' whose 'worn fingers scrabbling/At a torn sky ... stands/on the edge of everything'.

Another marginal figure is the elderly woman in 'The Widow of Kinsale', whose astringent sensibility is perfectly caught in fourteen terse, irregularly rhymed trimeters. Like the paperweight that sits on Mahon's desk, there is something obdurate and resistant about the speaker as she ruminates on her passionate past and dispassionately assesses her present circumstances. Indeed, she consciously compares herself to 'a rock exposed to the sun,/sardonic, cold and stiff,/I go with the ebb of life.' The half-rhyme of 'stiff' and 'life' jars uncomfortably and enacts the old woman's physical decline .The more she probes her past the more she sees how her 'once sexy self' has been replaced by 'nothing but skin and bone'. As so often in Mahon's poetry, the shoreline provides the *mise-en-scène* for private meditations. Despite 'the salt surge in my veins' she notes 'the shrinking sea' and concludes, wistfully, 'no more high tide for me'. The poem ends with a glimpse of peewits running on the strand and a vision of her own imminent incorporation into a dehumanised nature. We are reminded of Wordsworth's 'A slumber did my spirit seal', where the dead Lucy is 'rolled round in earth's diurnal course/With rocks and stones and trees'. Wordsworth's pantheistic *sangfroid* in the face of death, however, is not quite achieved by the speaker in 'The Widow of Kinsale'. The evening light may be warming the shore but the sea is far out and the last image of the poem strikes a distinctly chilling note:

> the ebb tide withdraws
> with a chuckle of bony claws.

Low and high tide, ebb and flow – Mahon's poetry in *Harbour Lights* oscillates between polarities. We move, for example, from the self-effacing haikus of 'Basho in Kinsale' – brief, lapidary observations from a Zen poet uprooted to the Irish coast – to the more sustained nature notes of 'Sand Studies'. In this poem Mahon returns to the question of representation, using the lexis of photography to bring the shoreline into sharper focus:

> These photographs, these
> vitreous transparencies

expose each bare feature:
original rock sculpture,
rubble and ropes of cream
as graphic as any dream.

Mahon not only sees each 'bare feature' but also listens
to each one. The ripples of the incoming tide, for example,
are heard as 'silent strings' while the vocabulary of music –
'thoughtful stave', 'blue note', 'soul breeze' – is deployed
to recreate a soundtrack to the 'raw reality' of the shore.
He discovers 'a new kind of "found"/spirit-breathing
music:/not pop, please, but the basic/tones of an ancient
sound'. The rejection of 'pop' is part of a wider resistance
to the 'bums and money' world of modernity. In its place
Mahon advocates an essential modesty, an ecology of the
self that allows the self to face its own annihilation:

You want a serene old age?
Cold front and icy ridge,
briny bubble and squeak
and the tributary leak
are waiting for you here

The world of the shore is emptied of human contents,
leaving it free for 'the fresh exposure/of a single sea
anemone' – again the language of photography – and the
'flick of a wren-wing'. As so often in Mahon's work, the
bird acts as an emblem of the poet himself, a singular figure
who 'sits on a rock to sing.'

'New Wave' continues that exploration of surface and

reality already begun in 'Resistance Days'. Instead of photography, however, it is film that provides the context for reflection, reflection itself being a key *leitmotif.* The title of the poem embraces both the *nouvelle vague* of French cinema – exemplified in the film that the poem reconstructs – and the wave which the young couple, the stars of the film, 'climb back into' at the end of the poem. It is a haunting image, raising questions about birth, death and the filmic, phantasmagorical nature of the life in between. The 'sandy prints' of these 'orphans going home' are temporary impressions, traces quickly erased by time and tide. The poem is a kind of storyboard, an elliptical narrative that hints at a love affair in a hotel on the coast, where the mood-music is 'the vague sorrow between man and woman', the word 'vague' subtly pointing back to the poem's title.

It could be any art film of the period, such is its generic nature. It is, however, carefully contextualised in the first stanza. We see the setting up of equipment, the coffee cups on the round tables, the actors preparing for their roles. We are made aware of the surface reality of the world they inhabit:

> from ice buckets, from windows, watches, knives,
> life flashes back at them their glittering lives.

The word 'glittering' suggests both cinematic glamour and the effects of artificial lighting. The couple see themselves in a reflected light, just as in 'Courtyards in

Delft' the young Mahon saw the coal 'glittering in its shed'. In addition, Mahon does not allow us to forget the artifice, the technology, that makes the production of art possible. He shows us the hand-held camera as it 'looks for natural light' and the mikes that 'pick up traffic and incidental sound'. Appearance and reality. As in 'Rathlin', we find ourselves among 'pitching surfaces', unsure of what is real and unreal, the only certainty being the 'snow of foam' into which the anonymous couple finally disappear as the film and the poem fade out.

The next two poems, as printed in *New Collected Poems*, rework the Homeric myth of Odysseus in a way that invites an openly biographical reading. Mahon had been separated from his wife for several years and was now living with a new partner. Maisie, his daughter, was born in 2003. In the same year he moved to Kinsale. The restlessness and personal upheaval of this period find their way into 'Circe and Sirens' and its companion piece 'Calypso'. It is impossible not to see in the island-hopping figure of Odysseus a thinly veiled self-portrait. Mahon/Odysseus is a man of no fixed abode, haunted by memories of his former life with Doreen/Penelope. They are poems about home and its unattainability. The sirens in 'Circe and Sirens' offer the 'agitated and wild-eyed' Odysseus a relaxed alternative – 'Odysseus, slow down!' – to the effortful striving of the conventional hero. We can perhaps see in this a validation of the feminised sensibility he had explored in 'The Cloud Ceiling'. Why, the poem asks, endure the

psycho-sexual trauma of an old, worn-out relationship
when one might experience the 'erotic weather' of a new
one? Why should Odysseus live up to some exhausted
notion of masculinity when 'he might retire, sea music in
his ears,/this micro-climate his last resting place,/and spend
his old age in sublime disgrace.'?

'Calypso' continues the argument. The misogynistic
demonising of women – the 'toxic cup, shape-shifting
witcheries' of Circe – is replaced by a genuine eroticism as
Calypso 'welcomed him with open arms and thighs,/
teaching alternatives to war and power'. The seduction
scene is described in language that draws attention to its
own sensuality:

> A wild girl rushing to the head like wine,
> she held him closely with her braided coils,
> her swift insistence, aromatic oils,
> her mild, beguiling glance, tuning his days
> to a slow sea rhythm; and through a salty haze
> he watched her moving as in a golden shower
> or swimming with her nymphs from the seashore.

Hugh Haughton is surely right in seeing 'Calypso' as an
anti-war poem. It is, specifically, both a statement of dissent
from the 2003 Bush/Blair doctrine of military intervention,
and an eloquent argument for feminist values:

> He prayed for an end to these moronic wars,
> burned wasteful sacrifices to the vague stars
> and dreamed of honey, yoghurt, figs and wine

> on night beaches, far from the life he knew,
> silent, unlit, but a faint murmur; a faint glow.

A veteran of the gender wars, Mahon surveys the wreckage of his marriage with a rueful sense of culpability. In another variation on the theme of exile, he writes of his 'brisk departure from the family home' and its legacy of 'desolation and long remorse'. Mahon, however, is in no hurry to return to Ithaca, and deliberately puts the word 'home' in inverted commas, preferring to linger in that 'cave house behind the dunes/enchanted now by hazel and sea-grey eyes'. Calypso's sexuality is strongly emphasised and leads to a reversal of values. The 'redemptive power of women' is now 'the important thing'.

That Mahon's failed marriage has left a bitter taste is clear from the remark that 'much-sought Penelope in her new resolute life/has wasted no time acting the stricken widow', the word 'acting' constellating a multitude of painful feelings. A sense of weariness enters the poem as Mahon describes the aftermath of his departure. The 'competing suitors' who suddenly appear in his absence do not provoke a violent response. He has 'no more heart now for a fight', a very unheroic reaction. Instead he lives a life of 'perpetual summer/stuck in a rock-cleft like a beachcomber', keeping his distance from 'home'. This is, I think, a significant moment. The quest for home, so long a paradigm of Mahon's work, is quietly abandoned with a shrug of the shoulders. The concept of 'home', a once-useful term but now a barrier to a deeper sense of belonging, of being in the world, is demystified. As in 'Sand Studies' the poem moves towards a greener vision of life in all its multiplicity. He becomes 'intent on pond life, wild flowers and wind play/the immense significance of a skittering ant,/ a dolphin-leap or a plunging cormorant.' He renounces the pursuit of power and macho posturing, an abdication of responsibility that sees him become 'an ex-king and the first philosopher in Greece'. The poem ends with Odysseus/ Mahon 'listening to voices echo' and 'still questioning that strange, oracular face', moments of quiet contemplation that rescue the hero from his own misplaced heroism.

The final poem, 'Harbour Lights', is a triumph of synthesis, weaving together the strands of a lifetime's thought and practice. This interior monologue – a *vade mecum* around the harbour port of Kinsale – gains its strength from being situated in the real time of global politics. The calm of the evening is heightened by the knowledge of what 'the Bush gang' are doing in the Middle East. War, however, is only the most extreme manifestation of a world that is, as Wordsworth said, 'too much with us'. Wordsworth's rejection of commodity culture – 'Getting and spending, we lay waste our powers' – is not far from Mahon's:

> for ours is a crude culture dazed with money,
> a flighty future that would ditch its granny.

The aptly chosen word 'crude' – as in 'crude oil' –

suggests the possible *casus belli* of the Iraq invasion, while the slant rhyme of 'money' and 'granny' sets up a disturbing juxtaposition. Later in the poem Mahon describes the present moment as 'the new dark ages'. The phrase encompasses not only military follies but the post-modern consensus of an information culture where 'everything is noticed, everything is known'. Mahon laments the fate of his cherished clouds, whether they are the abstract ones that enable poetry or the 'real' clouds above Kinsale:

> I toy with cloud thoughts as an alternative
> to the global shit storm that we know and love,
> but unsustainable levels of aviation
> have complicated this vague resolution;
> for even clouds are gobbled up by the sun,
> not even the ethereal clouds are quite immune:
> these too will be marketed if it can be done.

Mahon's non-compliance with a culture that would market the clouds if it could takes the form of a deeper immersion in the natural world. In the course of the poem Mahon gives us, *inter alia*, rabbits, foxes, midsummer light, hazel trees, larks, clouds, a 'tough/chough cursing you from a lichen-speckled roof', coves, beaches, the sea, orchards, wasps, flies, fresh flowers, pebbles, 'moon and pines', water, waves, rocks ... The poet, returning to the sea, climbs into the waves in the non-digital knowledge that 'everything is water, the world a wave'. Mahon is literally in his element as he asks, not entirely rhetorically:

Will the long voyage end here among friends
and swimming with a loved one from the white strands,
the sea loud in our veins?

We are back in 'A Swim in Co Wicklow', experiencing the 'hissing wash' of water or 'The Cloud Ceiling' where life begins with 'An ocean-drop'. At the end of 'Harbour Lights' a Darwinian struggle to survive is enacted in water, a struggle which one could relate to Mahon's own difficulties in finding *le vrai lieu.*

Down there a drenching of the wilful sperm,
congenital sea fight of the shrimp and worm
with somewhere the soft impulse of a lover,
the millions swarming into pond and river
to find the right place, find it and live for ever.

10

Life on Earth (2008)

MAHON'S LATE FLOWERING CONTINUED after *Harbour Lights* with two volumes in as many years: *Life on Earth* (2008) and *An Autumn Wind* (2010). Here, clearly, was a poet 'on form', not content to stand still or sink into a dignified dotage. 'Old men ought to be explorers,' said Eliot in *East Coker* and Mahon is emphatically an explorer in these two books, taking his increasingly green poetics as far as possible. In the interests of economy I shall restrict discussion in this chapter to a few key poems from *Life on Earth* and then flag up in the conclusion those poems from *An Autumn Wind* which would repay further scrutiny, had we but world enough and time.

Life on Earth begins with the by now familiar attempt to locate the source of creativity in writers with whom, for formal or personal reasons, Mahon sympathises:

Coleridge, Chekhov, Brian Moore. Coleridge, in particular, has long been an important presence in Mahon's poetry, a poet whose probing of the origins of art and his struggle with addiction find a parallel in Mahon's own work and peripatetic life. In 'Biographia Literaria' he identifies with the child who takes 'long solitary cliff walks,/cloud thoughts unfolding over the Quantocks', while in the poet's Aeolian harp – lodged in an open window to catch the 'corresponding breeze' – Mahon finds a symbol for the poetic genius, whose windchime sensitivity is the necessary pre-condition of art. The wind is an emblem of divine inspiration (we recall a similar trope in 'Beyond Howth Head'), and the young Coleridge experiences a moment of intense pleasure – the 'miracle' – when his laudanum-fuelled reveries translate into the realisation of 'Xanadu':

> Receptive, tense, adrift in a breezy trance,
> the frame is seized as if in a nightmare
> by some quotation, fugue, some fugitive air,
> some distant echo of the primal scream.
> Silence, dead calm, no worldly circumstance;
> the words form figures and begin to dance –
> and then the miracle, the pleasure dome,
> the caves of ice, the vibrant dulcimer.

The light phonetic step from 'fugue' to 'fugitive' (and later to 'figures') establishes the connection between art, flight and the ephemeral that we noted in 'Resistance Days'. We see Coleridge's poem materialising before our eyes, a product of the 'primary' imagination, a manifestation, as Coleridge believed, of the Mind of God. However, the 'wide-eyed sublimities of ghost and *Geist*' soon give way to weather reports, relationships real and imagined, Highgate Grove as a 'destined harbour' for the Ancient Mariner – an alter ego for Coleridge himself – and the poet's reincarnation as a '"sage/escaped from the inanity", aghast/ at furious London and its rising smoke,/the sinister finance of a dark new age'.

The prophetic, almost apocalyptic, language is reminiscent of Ruskin, another 19th-century sage, whose diatribes against the 'machine' find an echo in Mahon's conservative aesthetic. It was Ruskin, too, who coined the word 'illth' to signify all that is the opposite of wealth: poverty both material and spiritual, ugliness in the arts, the despoliation of nature. In Volume I of *Modern Painters* Ruskin includes an essay 'Of Truth of Skies'. His minute attention not only to skies and clouds but to natural phenomena of all kinds – flowers, ferns, trees, rocks, lichen, water, the wing of a bird – show that he was, like Hardy, 'a man who used to notice such things':

> If in our moments of utter idleness and insipidity, we turn to the sky as a last resource, which of its phenomena do we speak of? One says it has been wet; and another, it has been windy; and another, it has been warm. Who, among the whole chattering crowd, can tell me of the forms and the precipices of the chain of tall white mountains that girded the horizon at noon

yesterday? Who saw the narrow sunbeam that came
out of the south and smote upon their summits until
they melted and mouldered away in a dust of blue
rain? Who saw the dance of the dead clouds when the
sunlight left them last night, and the west wind blew
them before it like withered leaves? All has passed,
unregretted as unseen; or if the apathy be ever shaken
off, even for an instant, it is only by what is gross, or
what is extraordinary; and yet it is not in the broad
and fierce manifestations of the elemental energies,
not in the clash of the hail, nor the drift of the
whirlwind, that the highest characters of the sublime
are developed. God is not in the earthquake, nor in
the fire, but in the still, small voice.

That small voice can be heard throughout the two
sequences in *Life on Earth* – 'Art Notes' and 'Homage to
Gaia'. These poems take us back to one of the central
dialectics of Mahon's poetry: the tension between artifice
and, for want of a better word, reality. What is interesting
about late-phase Mahon is the relative ease with which
he discards the aestheticism that informed some of his
earlier poems in favour of a Ruskinian devotion to
'things'. This delight in materiality has always been there
of course. There is, for example, the recycled matter of
'Lives', the lost hubcap of 'The Mute Phenomena' and
the piled up rubbish behind the store-front facade in 'A
Garage in Co Cork.' However, this attention to objects,
whether man-made or natural, has always gone hand-in-
hand with an equally firm commitment to aesthetic values,

as we saw when looking at *The Snow Party* and *The Yellow Book*. Now, though, Mahon is less likely to be found kicking off his shoes and reading the Symbolists or 'proclaiming a different order of reality' as he contemplates the snowman in Hangover Square. Reality is increasingly wearing the look of the everyday.

The position is made clear in the third poem in the *Art Notes* sequence: 'Studio in Antibes', where Mahon adopts the persona of the painter Nicholas de Staël:

> 'Here I renounce abstraction, turning again
> to the world of objects, to the stoical souls
> of candlesticks and jugs, bottles and bowls.'

Later, he confesses that 'paint can't give me what I need to know', a point developed in the next poem 'Cushendun in Winter', a tribute to the Irish landscape painter Maurice Wilks:

> Wilks never bothered with 'the picture plane',
> with 'colour values' and the fancy words –
> as for aesthetics, that was for the birds.
> They slept in a yellow trailer at Shane's Cairn
> where, every morning, he would paint the world:
> hedges, fields, the sunlight on the river,
> the forest and the dunes, a still unspoiled
> paradise we thought would last for ever.

Painting the world. This could almost be a summary of Mahon's late-flowering verse, in particular of 'Homage to Gaia', the second sequence of poems in *Life on Earth.* It leads ineluctably to a quasi-religious devotion to Gaia, the great Mother of all, the personification of Earth herself, a figure hitherto seen most vividly in 'The Globe in Carolina'. In the title poem, 'Homage to Gaia', Mahon goes out of his way to demonstrate his green credentials:

> Since we destroyed the woods
>   with crazy chainsaws, oiled
> the sea, burned up the clouds,
>   upset the natural world
>
> to grow fat, if I may
>   I want to apologize
> for our mistakes and pay
>   homage to seas and skies,
>
> to field and stream: to you
>   great Gaia our first mother
> with your confused retinue
>   of birds, your weird weather.

What stops the poem from descending into green propaganda is, of course, the formal control, the technical mastery, particularly in the handling of rhyme and half-rhyme, the variation in the metre, the use of masculine and feminine line endings, the surprising lexis. Take the word 'retinue' in the line 'the confused retinue/of birds'. It is aptly chosen, evoking ideas of service, relationship and dependency, ideas wholly in keeping with the ecological argument of the poem.

Finally, before we look a little more closely at 'Homage to Goa', the stand-out poem of the collection, we should glance briefly at 'An Indian Garden', if only to register the increasingly eastern inflexion of Mahon's poetry at this time. Given his commitment to the recycling of materials, his own poems included, it is not surprising that Mahon should adopt a Hindu/Buddhist philosophy of change and decay. The (re)cycling of human lives, or reincarnation, takes place in the context of all life forms, the totality of nature:

> Indigo night fronds like
>   quills dipped in ink
> share in the life cycle
>   as quietly they drink
>
> the close tropical heat.

The poem goes on to explore the life cycle of a coconut from its transformation into a drinking bowl to its eventual fate as

> It rots in sandy soil
>   here at the ocean rim,
> changing to coal and oil
>   through geological time.

Mahon finds in these two examples – the frond and the coconut – analogues for human change, the cycle of birth and death, and ends with a flourish as he contemplates the 'spiritual substance' that 'rejoins the ancient dance' after our death. There is an echo here – a reprise – of the 'spirit-breathing music ... the tones of an ancient sound' that Mahon heard on the shoreline in 'Sand Studies'. The poem ends with another recycling of earlier material as Mahon, quoting himself, revisits the ending of 'Harbour Lights':

> It never really dies
>
> but circulates at random
>   somewhere in the ether
> when body closes down;
>   and so we live for ever.

The idea of circularity, of going round and round in a cosmic dance, is brilliantly realised in the image of ceiling fans at the beginning of 'Homage to Goa', the last poem in *Life on Earth*. Mahon establishes the Indian setting with references to the Hindu gods, ripe fruit and the ubiquitous mosquito:

> The ceiling fans in the house go round and round
> as if to whisk us off to a different sky.
> I squirt Deet at a thin mosquito whine;
> gods chuckle softly from a garden shrine;
> fruit ripen in the gloaming without a sound.

Mangos and mysticism: the poem is heterogeneous in its random mixing of elements. Mahon is just one feature in the scene as he rocks on the verandah in the early evening, a reincarnated hippy from the sixties, but more significantly a man who in a previous life was a 'mozzie':

> A mozzie once myself, *I* buzzed and bit –
> but only foot and elbow, ear and knee.

As a karmic reward for his good actions, the mosquito is reborn, first as a 'cheeky monkey' (the phrase is both literal and idiomatic), then as a pupil of a 'half-mad sadhu/at Brahmin school', before finally realising the Self as the speaker of the poem, a human figure who is, and is not, Derek Mahon. This homage to Goa is also a homage to Gaia; it is another *vrai lieu* that allows Mahon to honour Nature in all her sublime biology:

> The clouds recycle and we spread like plants,
> waves smash on beaches for no obvious purpose
> except to deliver the down-to-earth palingenesis
> of multitudinous life particles. A porpoise
> revolves on the sky as if in outer space
> where we started out so many aeons ago.

In language that echoes 'Lapis Lazuli', the speaker asks whether 'the streaming meteor, is it dead or alive,/a deliberate thing or merely gas and stone?' For a moment Mahon's vitalism wavers, but he soon recovers his neo-Darwinian spirituality, returning to the concept of eternal return in a way that reminds us of Yeats's resolution, in 'A Dialogue of Self and Soul', to 'live it all again':

Given a choice of worlds, here or beyond,
I'd pick this one not once but many times
whether as mozzie, monkey or pure mind.
The road to enlightenment runs past the house
with its auto-rickshaws and its dreamy cows
but the fans, like the galaxies, go round and round.

Postscript

THE IMAGE OF THE FANS ROTATING at the end of *Life on Earth* is a fitting emblem with which to conclude this study of Derek Mahon's poetry, committed as it is to the ever-turning world of life on earth. There is of course much more to say about this hugely impressive body of work, other poems to consider. Mahon's most recent volume, *An Autumn Wind*, published in 2010, contains many fine poems: there is a further chapter in the Odysseus story –'Ithaca' – which sees the hero set down on his own island and not recognising it as 'home'; two poems about storms – 'The Thunder Shower' and 'After the Storm' – the first displaying a dazzling range of acoustic effects ('It rings on exposed tin/a suite for water, wind and bin'); a magnificent poem about a beached whale; an *envoi* in 'At the Butler Arms' to the kind of hermeticism – that 'wild hush of dedication' – which had exerted such a magnetic pull on Mahon in earlier life; sympathetic portraits of Synge – 'in search of old reality' – and James Simmons, poet, critic, song-writer, singer, who 'chose/ reality over art and pose'; a postcard poem from, of all places, Lanzarote, whose 'basalt rocks, boulders like meteorites/and, under the volcanoes, active furnaces' remind us of 'the origins of the arts'; four place poems under the title *Autumn Skies*, the second of which, 'A Country Kitchen', recommends in typical Mahonian fashion that 'devotion to the real things/of a clean-swept morning'; and finally, in 'New Space', a glimpse of that 'venerable ideal/of spirit lodged within the real' – as good a definition of Mahon's *ars poetica* as any.

A *New Collected Poems* came out in 2011 (the edition I have used for this book) and a *New Selected Poems* has recently appeared (2016), both volumes – as indeed most of Mahon's work – published by The Gallery Press in Ireland. Mahon's publications, however, are not limited to poetry. As one would expect from a writer committed to the recycling of raw materials, Mahon has long been attracted to the art of translation. Indeed, *Raw Material* is the title of one of his most recent books, featuring adaptations based on poems by, among others, Ovid, Propertius, the Chinese T'ang poets, Pushkin, Baudelaire, Rimbaud and Rilke. Other translated works have included the poet Philippe Jaccottet (*Words in the Air*), a version of 'Le cimetière marin' by Paul Valéry (included in *Harbour Lights*), and a wide range of work for the theatre, from

The Bacchae (after Euripides) to Racine's *Phaedra*. There is also a *Selected Prose* and a selection of literary journalism, both volumes testifying to Mahon's intellectual range and reach. It would take another book to do justice to all these complementary engagements.

And so we come, by way of conclusion, to one over-riding, nagging question: given the intellectual *élan* and intense readability of Mahon's poetry, why is it so relatively invisible? Mahon's work is, of course, well known in Ireland and in the small world of contemporary poetry, but his general profile remains surprisingly low. When Seamus Heaney died in 2013 there was a genuinely felt sense of loss at the death of a great and much-loved poet. Heaney had become part of the collective consciousness, 'famous Seamus', a Nobel laureate who appealed to those who don't usually read poetry. Heaney is a staple of GCSE and A level examination boards, but not, outside Ireland, Derek Mahon. Why is this?

A number of reasons suggest themselves. Firstly, Mahon is notoriously bad at self-promotion, preferring to stand apart from the poetry circus and let the poems speak for themselves; secondly, he is not Seamus Heaney; thirdly, the intertextual nature of Mahon's poetry can be a challenge for nervous readers; finally, there is in Mahon's work a perceived 'resistance' to dominant forms of culture, a conservative reluctance to embrace more experimental modes of writing. Mahon himself sums up the situation in 'New Space':

Tolstoy, who later disapproved
of opera, plays and novels, loved

doorknobs, utensils, toys and song,
the homespun that the peasants wore –
everything simple, strong and clean,
art that was modest, not a chore;
and rhyming verses, not too long,
that say exactly what they mean.

Without going so far as to disapprove of poetry, Mahon's perspective on his own work is essentially sceptical. There is a basic humility throughout his poetry which expresses itself in a polyphonic verse more interested in the identities that crowd his page than his own conflicted self. Mahon is less concerned with 'Art' – with 'monuments of unageing intellect' – than with registering the flow of vital energy, the 'sensual music', that pulses through nature and runs into the channels of song. One of his most recent poems, taken from the Hindi of the fictitious 'Gopal Singh', is simply called 'Recycling Song'. The last stanza is a good note on which to end:

Throw nothing out; recycle
the vilest rubbish, even
your own discarded page.
Everything comes full circle:
see you again in heaven
some sunny evening in a future age.

Acknowledgements

Anyone writing about Derek Mahon does so in the knowledge that the definitive work on his poetry has already been written: Hugh Haughton's exemplary study, *The Poetry of Derek Mahon* (2007). I am deeply indebted to this book for the sensitivity of its readings of individual poems as well as for its magisterial overview of such a wide and complex body of work.

I am also grateful to Alan Wall of Chester University for generously giving up his time to read the manuscript and make important suggestions for its improvement. His meticulous attention to the details of this study has made this a much better book than it would otherwise have been. Any errors of fact or judgement are, of course, my own.

Thanks are also due to Janet Davidson and Patrick Ramsey for their tireless editorial support.

This book is dedicated to my wife, Michèle, and our daughter, Hannah, who have supported my enthusiasm for all things Mahonian with patience and good humour.

Select Bibliography

Selected Poems (Oxford University Press) 1991

Collected Poems (The Gallery Press) 1999

New Collected Poems (The Gallery Press) 2011

New Selected Poems (The Gallery Press) 2016

Enniss, Stephen: *After the Titanic: A Life of Derek Mahon*
(Gill & MacMillan) 2014

Haughton, Hugh: *The Poetry of Derek Mahon*
(Oxford University Press) 2007

Andrews, Elmer (ed): *Contemporary Irish Poetry*
(Macmillan Press) 1992

Dawe, Gerald and Foster, John (ed): *The Poet's Place: Ulster
Literature and Society* (Institute of Irish Studies) 1991

Deane, Seamus: *Celtic Revivals* (Faber & Faber) 1985

O'Brien, Sean: *The Deregulated Muse* (Bloodaxe Books) 1998

Paulin, Tom: *Ireland and the English Crisis* (Bloodaxe Books)
1984

Quinn, Justin: *The Cambridge Introduction to Modern Irish
Poetry* (Cambridge University Press) 2008

Index

SELECTED LITERARY TITLES
from GREENWICH EXCHANGE

W.H. DAVIES
Man and Poet: A Reassessment

Michael Cullup

978-1-906075-88-0 (pbk)
146pp

Even though he was once one of Britain's most popular writers, the reputation of the poet and memoirist W.H. Davies has, in recent decades, gone into decline.

Davies's colourful early life as a hobo and a tramp – captured by his most famous work *The Autobiography of a Super Tramp* – and his apparently 'innocent' poems about nature, tales about the seamier sides of life, his experiences on the road and verse portraits of those characters he met there – has led to the Welsh poet being placed under the cosy heading 'Georgian'.

It has been a tag which does serious disservice to the tone, nature and ambition of Davies's lyrics.

As poet and critic Michael Cullup shows in this brief but insightful exploration of the entirety of Davies's output – the memoirs, the short stories as well as the poems – there was a more complex personality than the one suggested by his public persona. True, he was a figure at home with the Georgian literary world – Edward Thomas and Hilaire Belloc were close friends – yet he was also capable of impressing more avant-garde talents like Ezra Pound and Jacob Epstein.

In this bracing reappraisal Cullup judiciously undermines preconceived notions of Davies the writer to reveal a poetic imagination richer, more insightful, more thoughtful than that for which he is generally given credit.

RAYMOND CHANDLER

Anthony Fowles

978-1-906075-87-3 (pbk)
206pp

The position of Raymond Chandler in the pantheon of American letters has long been subject to much debate.

Naturally imbued with a literary sensibility Chandler helped to revolutionise the crime genre, bringing to it a colourful, hardedged vernacular allied to a modern social commentary.

Through the figure of private eye Philip Marlowe, Chandler created a contemporary knight errant whose not so picturesque adventures trudging the mean streets of Los Angeles helped to vividly define the moral dilemmas of a dark, uncertain mid-century world.

And yet ... can *The Big Sleep*, *Farewell, My Lovely* and *The Lady in the Lake* be considered 'literature'?

Author Anthony Fowles – who freely admits to writing half-a-dozen 'sub-Chandlerian' thrillers – brings to the discussion both the detached eye of the professional critic and the sympathetic understanding of the practitioner.

It is a background which allows Fowles to make a balanced, finely-nuanced contribution to the ongoing Chandler debate, refusing to relegate the noir master to the wilderness of 'genre writer' but equally avoiding outlandish claims of literary pre-eminence.

In circumventing the pitfalls and simplicities of 'either/or', Fowles places Chandler's achievements in a fully-realised context, enabling the reader to appreciate more deeply the peculiar strengths and limitations of the prose lyricist of the American mid-century.

SWEETLY SINGS DELANEY

A Study of Shelagh Delaney's Work, 1958-68

John Harding

978-1-906075-83-5 (pbk)
204pp

Shelagh Delaney rose to fame following the instant success in 1958 of her first play *A Taste of Honey*. Lauded as Britain's answer to the controversial French novelist Françoise Sagan, Delaney's work scandalised her home city of Salford but established her as one of the country's most original and exhilarating young playwrights during a period in theatre history when women writers were rare and acceptance hard to achieve.

Delaney has served as an inspiration to countless young artists down the succeeding years. Rock star Morrissey wrote, 'She has always been a part of my life as a perfect example of how to get up and get out and do it.' Novelist Jeanette Winterson claimed, 'She was like a lighthouse – pointing the way and warning about the rocks underneath.'

Sweetly Sings Delaney is the story of her first exciting decade as a writer when she not only produced challenging and dramatic work in prose and on stage but also collaborated with some of the most innovative film and documentary-makers of the decade such as Ken Russell, Tony Richardson, Lindsay Anderson, not to mention actor and fellow Salfordian Albert Finney during his first and only foray as a film director.

JOHN KEATS

Against All Doubtings

Andrew Keanie

978-1-906075-75-0 (pbk)
110pp

Having identified him as a sort of semi-educated little cockney chancer, Keats's contemporary reviewers savaged him in the pages of Britain's most influential magazines. High ambition, unaccompanied by high birth, and radical affiliations and liberal inclinations, made him an object of contempt to those of, or aping the opinions of, the literary Establishment. In the short term, he never stood a chance.

Long after his death, his reputation was eventually brightened by much more enthusiastic – if, as some have since argued, misguided – appreciations for his beautiful and powerful otherworldliness.

Later still, in reaction to Keats-lovers' gushing admiration, a much more worldly Keats has been written up – including some bracing insights that seem to owe something to his first reviewers. As Martin Seymour-Smith has said, 'Many privately regard [Keats] with a condescension that is more smug than they would like to admit.'

This largely text-focused study promotes the best energies of a more Romantic view of a key Romantic figure. Keats was inspired and ill. By the time of his death, his genius and tuberculosis had pressurised him into poetry. The best he had to offer – including searching and scintillating confidences concerning how to live one's life in this world of suffering, 'the Vale of Soul-making' – are more accessible to the reader with a taste for poetry than they are to the consumer of ideologically appropriate journalism or ostentatiously unemotional academic analyses.

SECOND WORLD WAR POETRY IN ENGLISH

John Lucas

978-1-906075-78-1 (pbk)
236pp

John Lucas's book sets out to challenge the widely-held assumption that the poetry of the Second World War is, at best, a poor relation to that produced by its predecessor. He argues that the best poetry that came out of the 1939-45 war, while very different from the work of Owen, Rosenberg, Gurney, and their contemporaries, is in no sense inferior. It also has different matters to consider. War in the air, war at sea, war beyond Europe, the politics of Empire, democratic accountability – these are no subjects to be found in the poetry of the Great War. Nor is sex. Nor did American poets have much to say about that war, whereas the Americans Randall Jarrell, Anthony Hecht and Louis Simpson, are among the greatest English-speaking poets of World War Two. Both Hecht and Simpson write about the Holocaust and its aftermath, as do the English poets, Lotte Kramer and Gerda Mayer. For these reasons among others, English-speaking poetry of the Second World War deserves to be valued as work of unique importance.

A. E. HOUSMAN

Spoken and Unspoken Love

Henry Maas

978-1-906075-71-2 (pbk)
978-1-906075-73-6 (hbk)
61pp

A Shropshire Lad by A. E. Housman is one of the best-loved books of poems in English, but even now its author remains a shadowy figure. He maintained an iron reserve about himself – and with good reason.

His emotional life was dominated by an unhappy and unrequited love for an Oxford friend. His passion went into his writing, but he could barely hint at its cause. *Spoken and Unspoken Love* discusses all Housman's poetry, especially the effect of an existence deprived of love, as seen in the posthumous work, where the story becomes clear in personal and deeply moving poems.

ERNEST DOWSON

Poetry and Love in the 1890s

Henry Maas

978-1-906075-51-4 (pbk)
978-1-906075-73-6 (hbk)
48pp

Ernest Dowson is the archetypal poet of the 1890s. His best work comes entirely from the decade, and he died at the end of it.

Steeped in the Latin poets of antiquity and French 19th-century poetry, he developed an individual style which pared down the exuberance of Poe and Swinburne to a classical simplicity marked by meticulous attention to sound and initiating the move to more informal verse, which made his work attractive to the generation of D.H. Lawrence, Pound and Eliot.

His life was archetypal too. Born to respectable wealth and comfort, he was dragged down by family misfortune. His father's business failure and early death, his mother's suicide and his own advancing tuberculosis began the decline. It was hastened by drink and an impossible love for a young girl who never began to understand him.

In the end Dowson, the poet admired by Yeats, Wilde and a host of contemporaries, was reduced to living little better than a tramp in Paris, to die at thirty-two almost a pauper and alcoholic in a London workman's cottage, leaving posterity some of the finest love poetry in English.

BETWEEN TWO WORLDS

A Survey of Writing in Britain, 1900-1914

Hugh Underhill

978-1-906075-55-2 (pbk)
188pp

In 1924 Philip Gibbs, one of the first 'war correspondents' in the modern sense, wrote in his book *Ten Years After: A Reminder*, 'One has to think back to another world in order to see again that year 1914 before the drums of war began to beat. It is a different world now . . . ' A certain popular view has persisted of the Edwardian and pre-war Georgian period as a kind of swan-song to a past elegance and grace, and one of pleasure and freedom from anxiety.

The reality, along with, for many, the leisurely pace and settled way of life, was not only one of great intellectual and artistic excitement, but also of unrest, change and controversy. The first section of this survey, 'Britain 1900-1914: Hope, ferment and the abyss', looks at the political, cultural and economic elements of that ferment and the strains evident in British society: the reaction against Victorian attitudes, the pressure for social reform, the campaigns for women's suffrage and Irish Home Rule, the stirrings of Modernism and the move towards social realism in literature and the arts.

Underhill vividly demonstrates how these forces fed into the writing of the period. In the second section of the book, the work of the major authors of the period, Bennett, Wells, Conrad, Forster, Lawrence, Joyce, James, Shaw, Synge, Yeats, Hardy and Edward Thomas, is critically surveyed.

This is followed, in the final section, by a resumé of the work and varying significance of other authors against which those major figures need to be seen.

OTHER TITLES OF INTEREST

STORY
The Heart of the Matter
Maggie Butt (editor)
978-1-871551-93-8 (pbk)   184pp

MATTHEW ARNOLD AND 'THYRSIS'
Patrick Carill Connolly
978-1-871551-61-7 (pbk)   204pp

MILTON'S *PARADISE LOST*
Peter Davies
978-1-906075-47-7 (pbk)   108pp

LIAR! LIAR!
Jack Kerouac – Novelist
R.J. Ellis
978-1-871551-53-2 (pbk)   294pp

JOHN DRYDEN
Anthony Fowles
978-1-871551-58-7 (pbk)   292pp

THE AUTHOR, THE BOOK & THE READER
Robert Giddings
987-1-871551-01-3 (pbk)   240pp

POETRY MASTERCLASS
John Greening
978-1-906075-58-3   142pp

DREAMING OF BABYLON

The Life and Times of Ralph Hodgson

John Harding

978-1-906075-00-2 (pbk)   238pp

WORDSWORTH AND COLERIDGE

Views from the Meticulous to the Sublime

Andrew Keanie

978-1-871551-87-7 (pbk)   206pp

POETRY IN EXILE

A Study of the Poetry of Auden, Brodsky & Szirtes

Michael Murphy

978-1-871551-76-1 (pbk)   270pp

ALEISTER CROWLEY AND THE CULT OF PAN

Paul Newman

978-1-871551-66-2 (pbk)   224pp

IN PURSUIT OF LEWIS CARROLL

Raphael Shaberman

978-1-871551-13-6 (pbk)   146pp

To find out more about these and other titles visit

www.greenex.co.uk